-I Can Do-
HARD
THINGS
with God

I Can Do
HARD
THINGS
with God

ESSAYS OF STRENGTH
FROM MORMON WOMEN

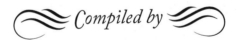 *Compiled by*

GANEL-LYN
CONDIE

with foreword by
RICHARD PAUL EVANS

Covenant Communications, Inc.

Printed in the United States of America
First Printing: February 2015

21 20 19 18 17 16 15   10 9 8 7 6 5 4 3

ISBN 978-1-62108-875-2

To my mom, Lou Ree
Thank you for doing the hard things of life with love and faith in God.

Acknowledgments

I WOULD LIKE TO THANK the following people for their support and assistance with this book.

Thank you to my supportive, amazing husband, Mr. Condie. You are the wind beneath my wings. My miracle children, Cameron and Brooklyn, I see you and know unconditional love. Thank you for being patient when my computer saw more of my face than you did.

Thank you to my amazing editor, Samantha Millburn, for giving this project watchcare from day one. Thank you for helping me believe that making a mistake didn't mean the end of the world, even when it felt like it. To the loving staff at Covenant, thank you for welcoming me with open arms. A huge thank you to Kathy Gordon for your vision and for helping bring these stories to life.

Foremost, I want to honor all the women who shared their honest, true stories of faith in this book. Your words will inspire readers to do the hard things of life *with* God. Laryssa Waldron, your intelligence and conversations with God were the blessings I needed at the perfect time. Thank you for helping with editing and fine-tuning to get this across the finish line! Betsy Ferguson, thank you for being part of our family and living your covenants even when life doesn't look like you thought it would. You are always a phone call away to comfort, counsel, and support. Elizabeth Harris, your story is honest and courageous. Linn Allen, thank you for your humor and faith and for totally getting it, sister. Kris Belcher, you helped me see the way God does; every time we are together, I am better for it! Kate Cowan, thank you for helping the world hear God. Liz Schultz, you were authentic at our first hello, and I will always love you for keeping it real when my own child was hurting. Lorraine Robinson Mason, I am blessed to be a part of your love story;

Kari wanted it this way from the beginning. Heather Jenson Hodge, you have been a friend, visiting teacher, and sister; now as a brilliant first-time writer, you can teach us all how to say good-bye to a child with grace. Carrie Ann Oscarson Rhodes, your humor and hope bring a new perspective on the pain of infertility. Andrea Palmer, I continue to learn from your counsel and strength. Alice Ann Weber, your story will bring healing to so many families; I want to be a mother like you when I grow up. Kylie Turley, your edit help was a beautiful gift, and your writing is a brilliant diamond in this crown of stories. Michelle Leonard, thank you for stepping out of your comfort zone, again, and adding so much to this project. Shelly Locke, your life is such an example of doing *great*, hard things with God. Barb Matthews, I wouldn't be a writer if it hadn't been for you. Thank you for believing in me first and helping fulfill a dream. I'm so happy we get to keep working together all these years later.

I want to thank my sister-friend Shawna Fillmore for the long talks through all of our wilderness experiences. Doing hard things with God is so much easier when He sends great friends who know my ugly and pretty sides. Jennifer Corrington, thank you for being there at the beginning of time and always thinking I am more than I see in myself. To Jenna Evans-Welch, Jen Thatcher, and Jan Tolman, a big thank you for edits, revisions, and more edits! Cheri Battrick, God sent you to us just in time! Your magic made more magic happen.

Richard Paul, your generous heart is my own "Christmas miracle" and has kept me moving forward when I've been tired and have wanted to give in. Your foreword is one of the most tender gifts I have ever received. Diane Glad, thank you for being a kindred spirit and an angel who believed in this manuscript to the very end.

God gives us ministering angels to comfort, heal, and support. Thank you, Nathalie Bowman, Holly Walton, D.d. Black, and Christine Anderson. You helped smooth out the rough edges along this three-year journey.

Finally, to my large extended family, you make it all worth it. Thank you for your support from this side of the veil and from the other! I miss you, Meg!

Contents

Part V: Mental Illness

Part VI: Alone but Not Lonely

Part VII: Doing More

Foreword
Richard Paul Evans

IN MY TRAVELS AROUND THE world, I often speak about loss and adversity. After one of my presentations, a newspaper reporter said to me, "What do you know about adversity? You have a charmed life." For a moment I just looked at him, then I replied, "You're kidding, right?"

The early years of my life were anything but idyllic. My mother suffered from severe depression and, on several occasions, attempted to take her life. My large family faced constant financial struggles. After my father broke both of his legs in a workplace accident, the ten of us moved into a three-bedroom duplex, and for two years I slept on the floor. In addition to my family's tribulation, I suffered with painful and embarrassing Tourette's Syndrome. Until the success of my first book, I suffered one business failure after another. For the first half of my life I felt everything around me was anything but charmed.

It took time, but through my adversity, I learned two great truths:

1. We do not succeed in spite of our challenges but oftentimes precisely because of them.

2. My Father in Heaven is near.

Life is difficult. Sometimes members of the Church are hesitant to accept this simple truth, as if worthy discipleship should make us immune to life's struggles. Indeed, this is not true. The Apostle Paul warned the Saints that they "must through much tribulation enter into the kingdom of God" (Acts 14:22).

I believe that in the premortal existence we were grateful for the opportunities we would have here on earth to become like our Father in Heaven—opportunities that would shape us, mold us, carve us, and refine us until we became more like Him. We knew, or were told, that these experiences wouldn't be easy but that they were necessary for our growth.

We accepted them in faith. But we couldn't understand how difficult our challenges would be until we put on this body of flesh and touched the flame. That is one of the primary reasons we came to this earth: to learn through our experiences good and evil, pleasure and pain, what our Savior faced.

Sometimes, in the throes of our suffering, it is easy to forget that pain isn't always a divergent path but rather the very road we must tread to salvation. Sometimes we want to give up. Sometimes we lose hope. But we cannot. That is what this book is about: hope. That is also what motivated Ganel-Lyn to compile these stories.

An author once told me that at its deepest level every book is really about its author. This book is no exception. When I first met Ganel-Lyn, who at the time was a reporter for a local magazine, I was impressed by the softness of her spirit. Through our acquaintanceship I learned that she had suffered great challenges in her own life—the kind of struggles that for disciples of Christ create a gentle soul. I don't believe it was a coincidence that Ganel-Lyn was inspired to write this book.

The Russian author Dostoevski said, "There is only one thing I dread: not to be worthy of my sufferings."[1] Suffering is a universal condition. If we are wise, we will face our suffering with Him who has endured all suffering. And in so doing come to know Him. Life is hard, but there is nothing too hard for God. He is all wise. He is all loving.

It is my hope that this book will increase your faith that God loves each one of us and is mindful of all we do and endure. And in spite of our weakness, with our Heavenly Father's infinite wisdom and power, we can do *all* hard things.

---

1 Viktor Frankl, *Man's Search for Meaning* (2006).

Good timber does not grow with ease,
The stronger wind, the stronger trees.
The further sky, the greater length.
The more the storm, the more the strength.
By sun and cold, by rain and snow,
In trees and men good timbers grow.

Douglas Malloch, "Good Timber," (May 5, 1877–July 2, 1938)

Introduction

I LOVE PARABLES AND WORD pictures. My children laugh at me because I am always drawing comparisons in life. Maybe I gravitate to this method of processing because it's how the Savior taught.

One of the most familiar allegories found in the scriptures is that of the olive tree and the master of the vineyard in the Book of Mormon. People often compare this story to missionary work and the gospel rolling forth, but one day as I studied these chapters, I was struck with a new personal insight. The words of Jacob 5:11 impacted me profoundly: "And the Lord of the vineyard caused that it should be digged about, and pruned, and nourished, saying unto his servant: It grieveth me that I should lose this tree; wherefore, that perhaps I might preserve the roots thereof that they perish not, that I might preserve them unto myself, I have done this thing."

Suddenly I saw that the gardener is God and I am the tree. The Master Gardener knows the strength of my roots, even when my life appears diseased and broken. He will allow the pruning and digging about so nourishment through the Spirit can restore a stronger, fruit-bearing tree. It was in that moment that *I Can Do Hard Things with God* was first realized.

These stories of faith are from women in the midst of their own hard things. The women are being pruned by the Master Gardener, and the pruning hurts. The stories are honest and painful, but they are also full of faith. They express great sorrow, but most of all they are full of hope. Each story highlights a different season of life and an acceptance of a disciple's path. Each illustrates how the pruning process refines, sanctifies, and strengthens. These women share their stories, and because of that, our hearts are connected and we become a Zion people. Together, we can do hard things with God no matter the disease, digging, or pruning we individually experience.

Part I: Hard Things

1

Suicide: No More Hiding

by Ganel-Lyn Condie

BEN FOUND OUR SISTER DEAD.

Meggan took her own life in our parents' backyard. There was no more hiding from suicide.

It was after 7:00 p.m. when my brother went to check on her at the Northern California home because my mom and stepdad were with me in Utah on the last day of their vacation. They were driving back home in the morning.

Meggan's teal blue Scion had been parked in the driveway for a few days. She must have been staying at their house while they were away. According to the neighbors, Meg had wheeled the garbage cans out to the curb on trash day, almost a week earlier, but no one had seen any movement since. She had been isolating *again*, and she hadn't answered anyone's phone calls or door knocks for days.

It was my mom's birthday. We finished the cake and presents, the candles and congratulations, and topped off a peaceful, lovely day of celebrating her life. After the festivities, everyone headed toward their individual rooms and settled down for the night. I went upstairs and turned out the lights, thinking I was the last until I heard movement in the kitchen and the sound of a door handle. I found my stepdad, Daddy Jim, coming in from the garage and knew instantly that something was wrong. It was like a bowling ball smashed into my heart, then fell with a thud to my stomach. "Dad?" I asked. "Dad? Dad?"

He walked so slowly to me. It felt more like we were swimming toward each other through the thick kitchen air. Then he said, "Ben called; there has been an accident."

I remember screaming, knowing already. "*No*! No, Dad! Bring her back! No, is she dead? Is it Meg?" But I didn't need to ask. I already knew.

He gently hugged me. "Yes, Meg's gone. We can't bring her back."

It was *no* accident. But I couldn't say the word out loud. Suicide. Suicide. *Suicide*—such an ugly, final, painful word.

I started to plead with my dad and with God, as if my words would make it change. "I want her back. Make her come back, please!"

My dad nodded sadly at me, then whispered, "We need to tell your mom." In slow motion, the nightmare grew in my kitchen.

I stumbled hysterically up the stairs, calling for my mom to come. She met me at the top of the stairs. My chest was heavy as I tried to speak the words I knew would shatter my mom's heart. "Ben's found Meg. She's dead!"

My mom fell to her knees and cried out. The wailing I heard coming from my own voice startled me. Even as I write these words, I can feel the nausea, the physical force that crumpled me beside my mother that night. I cannot replay the scene in my mind without tears coming to my eyes. Crawling down the hall to my daughter's room, I cried and mumbled, trying to explain to her what we had just discovered. Then I stumbled to the basement, where my son was already in bed. I choked on the words. "Aunt Meg . . . Meg is dead."

Looking back on that night, I see I had no business speaking to anyone, but I kept busy walking, crying, trying to make phone calls to my siblings, my father living in California, my stepmother, and my friends. That was what big sisters did; they took care of things, of everyone. I couldn't breathe, but I was trying to do my part.

My nightmare was real. My baby sister, the sweet girl I wanted to protect, was gone!

Why? Why? Why?

The question crept out of every sentence, hid under every word. Everything was stamped in my memory harder than concrete. I was hysterical.

For some reason, certain details seemed important to understand: We learned later that Meggan had already been gone for a few days when Ben found her body. The decomposition had made it difficult for them to identify her. Specifics about how she died kept me awake for months; they still do. The thought of my Meg alone and outside brings waves of pain washing over me, crashing over me again. Why? Why now? Why this way? Why couldn't I save her? Why didn't she ask to be saved?

* * *

Grief is hard no matter the loss, and I do not minimize anyone's pain, but suicide is a grief all its own. No matter how you try, you can't hide from the monster web of emotions, the tangled knot of questions. It can't be avoided, downplayed, or minimized. It knocks the wind and sometimes even the faith out of the strongest of God's disciples.

For days and weeks and months following that horrific night, I felt out of control, and control has always been my mode of operation. Multiple loved ones in my family deal with mental illness, and this fact has always kept me on guard. Watching my little sister fight for her life through forty years of depression pushed me to be a bit of a control freak. Among other things, I wanted to protect and save Meg, to fix the things that hurt her, to control the circumstances, but in the end I couldn't. No one could—not her devoted bishop or caring therapist, not her attentive visiting teachers or her countless friends and family who adored her. She took her life. She was gone.

* * *

Something changed in me when I found out about Meg, and I knew it would never leave and I'd never be the same again. The pain was suffocating. Was my faith lacking? Was I not spiritually prepared for such a grand loss? I knew the plan of happiness. I had been taught and shown through the power of the priesthood that she was okay and at peace. But I still hurt. I found that we as Latter-day Saints don't mourn very well *because* we know the plan. We mistakenly think we shouldn't hurt. So when Meg's suicide left me with a big, messy hurt that demanded to be mourned, I didn't quite know what to do.

During the first few weeks after her death, I was in shock. I didn't know how to be normal. I wrote her obituary and planned her funeral, but there were moments I felt like I was standing outside the scene, watching everything happen from afar. It is shocking to me that I was actually doing those things. I was grieving death but still trying to live. I felt like I was caught in a long, bad dream. Those first few days were filled with so much emotion that even taking a shower was difficult. I remember going to Walmart that first week following her death and noticing people in the store acting so normal. I had the urge to announce over the loudspeaker to everyone in the store that the world was different now because my beautiful sister was dead.

The devastation felt so immense. I remember asking in the months following, "What if I didn't believe in God? What if I didn't have the gospel? What if I didn't know about prayer or priesthood power? What would I do to survive this grief?"

Previous periods of pain and adversity had taught me there was always a gift involved. Faith in Christ had always led me to the treasures hidden within every personal trial. This time was no different. I was given three cherished gifts from the grief, but I didn't recognize them in the beginning weeks or months following Meggan's suicide. They came in the Lord's due time.

The first gift of grief I recognized was knowing I couldn't hide from God. I tried to hide from the grief I was feeling, but because I was a mom and others were dependent on me, hiding wasn't always an option. In the days following Meg's passing, I could feel her next to me, and though I wanted to go to her because I missed her so much already, I knew my earthly mission wasn't complete. Still, my heart and mind so often wanted to be with her. It took daily prayer, scripture study, and going to church no matter what to keep me grounded. My daily spiritual practices literally kept me alive. It also seemed so right to go to the temple the night before I left for Meg's funeral. The sadness was exhausting, but I went to fill my vessel with oil. I trusted the promises found in Doctrine and Covenants 109:22: "And we ask thee, Holy Father, that thy servants may go forth from this house armed with thy power, and that thy name may be upon them, and thy glory be round about them, and thine angels have charge over them." I had read that verse for strength before, but never had I needed it as desperately as I did then.

Even with angels beside me, I had to live through the grief and reality of what had happened. I hadn't lived close enough to my sister to care for her for more than twenty years, so I wanted to be the one to help her now, to be there for her so I could find closure. When I mentioned that I wanted to dress her body alone, everyone seemed worried. Even Craig, a friend who worked as a sheriff in California, called to tell me not to open the body bag. I felt strongly that I should care for Meg, like it was a last act of service and stewardship as her big sister, but at Craig's insistence, I agreed not to dress Meg, though I would not disobey the prompting either: I would visit her body and bring her clean garments and her temple clothing.

I prayed with my mom at the funeral home's reception area. With my husband on the phone from Utah, I prayed again. Then I went into the quiet holding room. Like a sacrament table, a white sheet was draped over the top of Meg's body bag. I cautiously touched her now cold, hard form. It was difficult to feel her through the layers, so I pressed more firmly until

I found her legs and feet; I rested my hand there. Finally, I opened her temple bag and removed a clean pair of garments and her temple dress. I draped them on top of the sheet covering her to symbolically dress her body, then I reached back into the bag and found two pair of nylons. Speaking out loud, I said, "Sister, I am leaving two pair of nylons in case one pair runs." I laughed and felt her spirit laugh with me.

The tears started to roll, and my emotions swelled as I pulled out her current temple recommend. As I wept by Meg's lifeless body, I saw so clearly that her entire life and the many good choices she had made allowed her to die with a current temple recommend. Suicide was about her final choice on earth, not the sum total of all she'd done. She had made countless good choices but only one final choice that had ended her mortal mission.

My tears kept dropping as I stood in the stale silence of the funeral home, and my thoughts returned again and again to Meg's lifetime battle with depression. It seemed to be her constant companion. We had spent hours on the phone talking about her divine worth; I'd pled with her to allow God's love in. But even then, the illness was too oppressive for her to overcome.

Standing there now, with Meg, I knew God's love was with us both. We weren't hiding from Father in Heaven. No matter how long it took to go to Him, I would make the journey, and I would find Meg waiting for me too.

The second gift of grief was the shocking reminder that I could not afford to hide from others. Some mornings I would wake up and pray just to be able to get out of bed. Then I would pray just to be able to open my scriptures. When I did this, I always found comfort and strength. Sitting quietly in meditation helped me find God, even through the numbing grief that clung to my soul. There were times when I'd let my heart start to harden and close up, thinking maybe then it would stop hurting. But God would send ministering angels both seen and unseen to help me open up again. The truth was apparent—I needed others to survive. I'm sure it was tempting for some to wait to do the *right* thing for me when I was hurting, but they always made the biggest difference when they just did *something*. God worked with anything they had to offer.

The night we found Meg, my dear friend Kolleen texted me Mosiah 3:11: "For behold, and also his blood atoneth for the sins of those who have fallen by the transgression of Adam, who have died not knowing the will of God concerning them, or who have ignorantly sinned." The Spirit comforted me through a friend and a simple scripture. It did not take away my grief, but a friend reaching out blessed me and continues to bring hope to my ever-healing heart.

One day, my sweet visiting teacher Jan came to minister to me. I hadn't been sleeping, and I was exhausted planning Meggan's funeral. Jan knocked on my door and said simply, "I can't do much, but I have something I want to give you." Sitting in my living room, and with a voice of an angel, she started to sing me her favorite hymn. Tears poured down both our faces as we held hands and her song spoke peace to my soul. She couldn't give me a magical potion to make it all better, but she gave what she had.

Months after the funeral, Shawna called to cry with me. She didn't fix anything; she just wanted me to know it was okay if I was still not feeling like my old self. My nephew Nate simply apologized for not checking on me more. I felt ministered to when my longtime friend Jen asked how I was doing and *really* wanted to know, even when there was nothing new to say. We think we are alone, but we never are.

Elder David A. Bednar taught, "I do not know why some people learn the lessons of eternity through trial and suffering—while others learn similar lessons through rescue and healing. I do not know all of the reasons, all the purposes, and I do not know everything about the Lord's timing. With Nephi, you and I can say we 'do not know the meaning of all things' (1 Nephi 11:17)."[2] In the days and weeks that followed my sister's passing, I came to know that healing was more like a slow cooker than a microwave. I am grateful for the Lord's timing. I was given the gift of people when God knew I needed it most, when I wanted to hide. It was so easy to want to isolate when I was struggling. Meg had falsely believed hiding from loved ones was the right thing to do, but we hurt more when we are alone. In retrospect, I see I was prepared for this hard thing; God tutored me for years about how not to be alone in my suffering. He wanted to make sure I knew before Meggan's death that I was never alone and that I shouldn't hide from others.

The third and greatest gift that came from Meg's suicide was the realization that I had broken parts but that I was not broken and worthless. I accepted that Meg had broken parts, but I wanted her alive anyway and with me always. Ironically, I struggled to accept my own imperfections. I wanted to hide them from God and from everyone. As a child, I falsely believed that if I was perfect and never made a mistake, the people I loved

---

2 "That We Might 'Not . . . Shrink' (D&C 19:18)," *CES Devotional for Young Adults*, March 3, 2013, University of Texas Arlington.

wouldn't be hurt or hurt me. I worked to be perfect in hopes that I could somehow save God extra work so He wouldn't have to help me too much. It sounds so odd to spell that out, but even now there are times I still mistakenly believe it is true.

After losing Meg, I had to stop hiding from myself and the truth: I was not perfect no matter how hard I tried. I would make messes. I would disappoint and hurt people even when I didn't mean to. I would fail. God knew it would be this way, and He gave me a Savior to die for me. I'd known these truths all my life, but I learned to feel them only after Meg died.

Even if I was a burden, God would remain God. He would take my lowly burdens and carry them easily forever. I didn't need to save Him work. Somehow I understood more clearly that my Father in Heaven was my father. When I was low, sad, tired, and imperfect, I could go to Him, and He wanted me to. He knew all my broken parts. Meggan's death taught me that I was imperfect by design but that God wanted me this way so I would turn to Him with humility and meekness. Then His grace would be made manifest through me.

Elder Bednar taught powerful truths about healing and faith: "Righteousness and faith certainly are instrumental in moving mountains—if moving mountains accomplishes God's purposes and is in accordance with His will. Righteousness and faith certainly are instrumental in healing the sick, deaf, or lame—if such healing accomplishes God's purposes and is in accordance with His will. Thus, even with strong faith, many mountains will not be moved. And not all of the sick and infirm will be healed. If all opposition were curtailed, if all maladies were removed, then the primary purposes of the Father's plan would be frustrated."[3]

* * *

Christ wept. He knew the plan, but He still wept with Mary and Martha when Lazarus died. So as I knelt by the open grave and lowered Meggan's ashes into the earth, I wept bitterly. Christ knew those tears. That little bit of gray dust was my sister, and I was holding her for the last time in this life. I thought of holding her as a baby for the first time. I was two, and she was a squished, red-faced baby born in an army hospital in Germany.

---

3 "That we Might 'Not . . . Shrink' (D&C 19:18)."

She was a bundle of joy, a pink-swaddled baby of softness that I could dote on and take care of. She was more than my baby sister; she felt more like my own baby, and I fell desperately in love with her. In my naïve little heart and with all the sincerity of a young child, I promised to protect her always.

Through the years, the trial of my faith has been learning how to better accept my own role. God saved Meggan. I was to love and support her. No matter how much I prayed over the years for her, she never experienced complete healing while she was on earth. I didn't have the power to heal her, but God did. Elder Spencer J. Condie said, "In this age of one-hour dry cleaning and one-minute fast-food franchises, it may at times seem to us as though a loving Heavenly Father has misplaced our precious promises or He has put them on hold or filed them under the wrong name. . . . When heaven's promises sometimes seem afar off, I pray that each of us will embrace these exceeding great and precious promises and never let go. . . . God will remember you."[4]

God remembers me, and He remembers Meggan, and He allows us to continue to strengthen each other. I often feel Meggan nearby, caring for me. One day I thought of her so powerfully while I was in the celestial room that I opened my eyes in the middle of my silent prayer, literally expecting to see her standing beside me, looking like an angel in her white clothing. At other times I have felt her patting my cheek at night while tears have wet my pillow. She has been there when I haven't seen her. And she, my darling sister, will rise again as Christ did. I know this to be true in unspeakable, deep ways. The great plan of happiness is almost tangible to me because I have felt the contrast of it with the hurt and grief I've experienced.

Life poses plenty of opportunities to hide, but if we, like Adam and Eve, use our agency to come out in the open to face God, to face our fellow man, and to face our inadequacies, we can be intensely strengthened. When an army is trying to take out a foe, their first objective is to knock out their enemies' communication tools and isolate them from the strength that comes from unity. I have learned that true strength and protection can come with these three gifts of grief. Despite my own adversities, my fears, my inadequacies, and my failures, despite Meggan's choice to leave this life by suicide and the aftermath that will stay with me all the days of my life, I testify that God will consecrate my afflictions for

---

4 "Claim the Exceeding Great and Precious Promises," *Ensign*, Nov. 2007.

my gain.[5] Faith allows tragedy to be transformed into treasure. He will do this for me, and I will continue to see His hand in the gifts He sends me as I do hard things with Him.

---

5 See 2 Nephi 2:2.

Part II: Health

2
Chronic Illness: An Essay about Being Sick. Very Sick. For a Very Long Time.
by Kylie Turley

GETTING SICK HAS CHANGED THINGS for me. I used to look in the mirror and see a competent, faithful, attractive woman who had much to offer; now I see a woman whose medication-induced thinning hair and deep wrinkles speak of pain and worry; a wife who offers her husband the onus of being unequally yoked with an increasingly disabled companion; a mother who needs her children to clean and cook and garden—not because of some well-developed child-rearing methodology but because she cannot do it herself; and a daughter of God who wonders what kind of Father would choose a life of pain for His beloved child. I have rheumatoid arthritis and Parkinson's disease, as well as medication side effects ranging from ringing ears and osteoporosis to extreme weight loss and migraines. How do I feel about that? It depends on the day. Some days I feel vulnerable, others angry, exposed, useless, tolerated, sad. I am a liability, a hindrance, a commitment. My purpose is seemingly to give others an opportunity to serve, and, frankly, that is a lonely, depressing way to live.

* * *

Phew. That last paragraph sounds maudlin. I have a rheumatologist, a neurologist, a neuro–ophthalmologist, a gynecologist, a dermatologist, and a movement disorder specialist on speed dial. Luckily, one of my sisters is a counselor, and one of my friends is a psychologist, though I probably ought to locate a neurosurgeon, occupational therapist, and internist—just to be safe. After all, my last MRI showed a 5.18 mm brain lesion, so there are a few things that could still go wrong.

"Well," I told everyone, "no surprise there. I have suspected brain damage for years. Don't you think it explains so much?"

That brings me to one of my primary coping methods: denial served with a dash of humor and a pinch of sarcasm. It is really quite useful. Health insurance and massive medical bills? Pshaw. Those nice politicians will get it all sorted out. Husband? Clearly, he adores me. And kids? No problem there; why would any child want a healthy mom? Unhealthy moms do not hover while you do chores, do not hound you to be overly involved in extracurricular activities, and do not see anything wrong with the whole family putting on their pajamas by 6:00 p.m. on Friday nights.

I particularly enjoy pretending that I might feel better tomorrow. Or at least next summer. And the future? I need not be concerned since it will doubtless be lovely. "Sufficient is the day" and all that stuff.[6] There is so much room in my life for healthy denial.

I have been in denial since my health fell apart seven years ago. If I heard my story, I would label me "hypochondriac" and move on, but be aware that I used to be perfectly healthy. Then I spent more than a year dealing with random finger joints swelling, foot pain, shoulder pain, knee pain, and other pains cropping up before someone thought of rheumatoid arthritis. Enter denial.

I spent the first six months whimpering biweekly to my sister. "I keep thinking this will just go away. How can I be sick? I am not a sick person. I don't even have a doctor. No one in our family is sick. All these forms say to list family illness, and I draw a straight line all the way down through no."

Most days I spun some bizarre spiritual denial as well. It went something like this: "God does not give us trials we are not capable of handling. I cannot handle having rheumatoid arthritis. Therefore, God will take it away."

Heavenly Father's ways are apparently not my ways.

I next tried spiritual bargaining, the "I will serve Thee all my days if Thou wilt cure me" kind of emotional appeal/deal, which obviously didn't work for me either. That might have been because I had already covenanted to serve Him years ago. Oops. Maybe I should have held out.

* * *

One morning, a couple months into the arthritis diagnosis, with four medications tried and rejected, I limped to breakfast, fell onto my pillowed

---

6 3 Nephi 13:34.

wooden chair, and stared at my bowl of lumpy oatmeal. Cradling my hurting right wrist with my swollen left hand, I felt tears squeak out and leave chilly trails down my cheeks. I glanced at my five children and their upset faces, then stood without a word and limped out. In my bedroom, I collapsed on the pillow-top mattress, unable to curl up in a ball because my knees and hips hurt. My husband came in, but I rolled over so my back was to him and kept crying. Over and over I whimpered, "I can't do this. I simply cannot do this. I can't."

The stupid thing about such moments is that they do not change a thing, but that still doesn't keep me from having them.

Personally, I believe in breakdowns, another strange mechanism I periodically pull from my coping arsenal. My sister-in-law, a type-1 diabetic since age eleven, told me she gave herself three days for every new crisis. It seemed like fairly good advice, so I tried it. Four years ago, when my left arm stopped swinging, I moaned for at least three days and whined to my husband that it threw me off balance and that I felt weird and that everyone was staring. Three years ago, when I lost sensation in my left foot, I took a day or two to mourn; I never knew how much I'd miss feeling the back sides and tips of my toes, not to mention the ticklish shock of touch on my instep, until I couldn't feel them anymore. To those of you who have not lost this, you should offer a prayer of silent gratitude right now for the sensation in your left foot.

A few years ago, my neurologist admitted that some of my symptoms might be Parkinson's disease but that she still wasn't sure since I was such an abnormal case. That called for a breakdown and some routine denial—I bawled all the way to my husband's office, demanded a blessing, then convinced my four-year-old daughter to spend the afternoon eating buttery popcorn and watching *Pride and Prejudice* with me. I knew I would have to adjust, to reconcile myself to the new loss, but I didn't have to do it that day.

The thought process is slightly irrational, but it helps. Everyone knows big blows take some adjustment, but so do the little ones.

* * *

With chronic illness, there is not just one big adjustment. I wish there were. I hate this slow deterioration, this constant corrosion, this creeping disintegration. I thought about it again when my neurologist reassured me that it would be very, very rare if my 5.18 mm brain lesion turned out to be a tumor. She spent a good fifteen minutes soothing me—explaining details, sizes, homogeneity, and the relative normalcy of "just one." I put on my serious face, but inside I was thinking a tumor might be easier. Fact: both my doctor and I know that if my next brain scan shows more lesions, we will start talking about multiple sclerosis. Most days I hold running conversations with God; today I said, "Really, Father? Not just one but three chronic, degenerative illnesses? I know Thou art holy and Thou art mindful of me and my best interests, but I am just wondering how this could possibly work out well for me or my kids or my husband or anyone else around me. Not that I am questioning Thee. Or Thy plan. I'm just saying."

* * *

A few months later, visiting at my parents' home, my seven-year-old son came to tattle on his older brother.

"Mom," he complained. "Christian is saying I'm a baby, and he won't let me play with him and our cousins."

I tried to listen patiently, though both the teasing and the resulting whining were habitual and annoying.

"Go tell him his mom wants to talk to him," I said in third-person omniscience.

My little boy gleefully trotted off, having accomplished his mission. My older son sulked in, defensive and abrasive, launching into an explanation before I could open my mouth.

I cut him off. "Honey," I said moderately, noticing my sisters were watching the interchange. "Can we just get along today? Can we all play nicely?"

He agreed and stalked out, still mad in spite of his verbal compliance. I had no doubt we would have the same conversation again shortly.

My sister stared at me, opened her mouth, closed it, then rocked back in her chair. "He came," she finally blurted out.

"What?" I inquired, knowing she was talking about one of my sons but not understanding her. Caid always tattled; Christian always teased. What was so surprising?

"Christian. He came. He knew you were going to get mad at him, and he came anyway."

He did. I was not astonished that he'd come. He always did. But my sister's surprise surprised me and made me think. In my regular tally, all my children lose by having a sick mom, but I should give credit where credit is due: *Okay, Father,* I thought. *I thank Thee for showing me one good thing about having RA. My children come when I call. They respect my pain enough to know I cannot chase after them and could never physically drag them off the playground equipment after four warnings about leaving a park. I am not conceding that this is going to work out well in any holistic sense, but I will give you that one, Lord. He came.*

* * *

Despite all of the talking I do with God, I really do not understand Him or the plan He has going for me. Religious people tell me all things happen for a reason, but that's rather tricky to deal with. All the spiritual stuff is. I doubt people mean to imply that I needed this particular lesson to humble and subdue my wicked nature, but they do. I also doubt they mean to suggest I could be healed if I just had enough faith, but they do. I have been told that I caused my illness and that I subconsciously want pain and illness in order to get attention. Personally, I think it is rude to say such things. I ignore them.

No one need say it anyway. It is not as if we chronically sick people do not wonder the same things and feel guilty all by ourselves.

* * *

If I let it, the guilt could gnaw my insides out, and so could the anger. I hate thinking that this year might be the last year I will slip my shirt on and off by myself or that this month might be the last month I will hold a fork and feed myself or that this time might be the last time I can force my fingers to unbuckle the baby's car seat.

I despise losing little things. Since my right wrist began hurting two years ago, I have been unable to chop crunchy, fresh vegetables no matter how sharp the knife or how much I love to eat them. I've written this entire essay using voice-activated software since Parkinson's means my left hand and fingers no longer obey brain signals very well. I am grateful that I can still walk, but my left foot drags a bit, and I abhor the uneven sound: click, scratch-click, click, scratch-click. A couple months ago, I had to have my husband shave my armpits. Trust me, *humiliation* does not begin to describe it, though my husband insists it is always his pleasure to help me bathe.

I've been losing the ability to do big things too: Labor Day 2007 was the last time I went rock climbing. I was afraid it might be, but all it took to confirm its finality was spending the next day in bed with excruciating pain, unable to count to ten unless I was lying perfectly still with heating pads tucked strategically around me. I then paid the price for the next two months with doctors' visits, steroid shots, and constant pain in places no one needs to know about. No, I will not be rock climbing again, not even on my best days.

The loss plays tricks with my mind. Hopeful, happy people probably have no idea how their ability to handle problems today comes from their belief that tomorrow will be better. At the same time chronic illness robs the present of ease and vibrancy, it makes a hopeful future nearly impossible to imagine. Can healthy people understand? The future weighs on me so much. Most days I really can handle the physical pain of arthritis and the shaking and slow movement of Parkinson's, but the knowledge that it is never going away makes it unbearable. Absolutely unbearable. I bend under the bulk, bowed by the burden, and wonder when the weight will snap me in two like a toothpick. Maybe I used to pride myself on facing reality with a cool, calculated stare and analytical logic, but I now know how *not* to think, *not* to plan, and *not* to organize. Thinking about the future is *not* allowed.

I have heard that living in the moment is a strength. That may be right, but it is a strength that takes some getting used to.

* * *

When I was first diagnosed with rheumatoid arthritis, I decided to deal differently with illness than I had with past problems. Typically, I would hide in my head and solve my problems in my own little world, then come out when I was ready. But I learned a new way from watching a friend deal with the death of her baby courageously and in full public view. I told family and friends openly, crying and admitting my frustration and my confusion. Word spread, and people with chronic illness sought me out to tell me, "The first year or two is the hardest, but you will be okay when you get stabilized with a medication that works for you." That helped. But, unfortunately, it didn't turn out to be true; I am just the weird one for whom medications do not work or cause bizarre and/or severe side effects. My diabetic sister-in-law recommended I add flexibility to my coping cache: "Do whatever it takes," she said, suggesting I feel free to whine, pray, laugh, cry, deny, embrace, ignore, fight, be still, take methotrexate or not, try acupuncture or yoga or not, go to a movie, read, or hold my breath. Or not. Whatever I needed. "When you are strapped into a roller coaster against your will, enjoy the view when you are up, scream when you are upside down, and close your eyes when you need to," she said. That makes more sense all the time.

I do not believe misery likes company, but it really helps to have people who understand. For most people, I show my "stiff upper lip" side, while a few close friends and family members get my "this is really hard" side. My friend with MS gets the morbid humor. She brought my family dinner—a nice, homemade lasagna and bread and salad—one night during my week of bed rest after a spinal tap gone wrong. The next day she called, laughing hysterically and nearly yelling into the phone, "You will never guess where I am. The hospital!" We giggled for fifteen minutes about coordinating hospital crises and the jittery feeling prednisone causes. My husband raised his eyebrows in deep concern as I wiped away tears and snorted at the hilarity of my suggestion to have him run the leftover lasagna back over to her family. For some reason, it is only funny when I'm talking to people in the same situation.

* * *

Sometimes, when people learn of my illnesses, they say things like, "You are going to learn to be so compassionate." That doesn't help. You don't have to believe me, but I know I'm right when I say that simply being in pain does not automatically teach empathy. In fact, often, it is just the opposite. It feels like someone is scratching coarse sandpaper up and down my temples when I hear people lament the pain of paper cuts and stubbed toes. My husband once looked at me with sad, bleary, puppy-dog eyes and mournfully intoned that he was "so sick of being sick," then he blew his nose like a foghorn for effect. I let the words hang in the air. For ten long, awkward seconds. Afterward, I told him I was sorry and that I hoped he would feel better soon. I managed not to roll my eyes. And, actually, I did hope he would soon get over his two-week cold; after all, someone had to take care of me.

I am exaggerating a little bit. It is true that I am much more aware now, aware that there have always been people around me who struggle with illness and difficulties. Before this happened, I was indecently ignorant of pain and distress. Remember when I said I didn't know anyone with rheumatoid arthritis? Turns out I was wrong; approximately one in every 100 people has rheumatoid arthritis, and I know thousands of people.[7] I have been surrounded by people with arthritis all my life—but I was too selfish to realize they had it. I was prone to judge someone who did not help take down chairs and wash dishes after the ward dinner or sign up regularly on the compassionate service list. Now I worry when I see people not participating. I want to know what's wrong and how I can help them. I never want to add to another person's pain if I can avoid it. No one needs me to add to their burdens.

If that is empathy, then maybe I am learning it.

* * *

One person spent a vigorous hour explaining to me that "despair cometh because of iniquity."[8] I tried to reason that just because despair "cometh . . . of iniquity," it doesn't necessarily mean it *only* comes from iniquity. I thought it was a nifty piece of logic, though I did not persuade my debating opponent. So label me "iniquitous" because despair is a short three or four sentences away almost every morning and at any given moment of the day. Just the electric jolt of my feet hitting the carpet after some of the thirty-three joints per foot have become swollen and inflamed in the night is enough to set me on the path to despair. Panic rings in my mind, the alto of my speaking voice laced with a high-pitched whine that tightens my back and shoulder muscles, clenches my teeth, and starts pressure building behind my eyes. I think:

1) If this is how I feel today, how will I feel tomorrow?

2) I already have to make my children twist the can opener, chop the vegetables, and scrub the floors; how will I manage when they are gone?

3) And when they return home, I will not be able to hold my sweet grandbabies, much less play with them as toddlers. I will be bedridden and helpless.

See? Despair—in three sentences. It takes a firm mind to stay focused in the moment, and sometimes it takes a half hour or so to convince myself that I really do want to get out of bed and get going.

Spiritual things would be less confusing if I didn't believe in a God of miracles. But I do. "If thou wilt," the leper said to Jesus, "thou canst make me clean."[9] The Lord was "moved with compassion" and touched the leper,

---

7 See "Rheumatoid Arthritis," Patient: Trusted Medical Information and Support, http://www.patient.co.uk/health/rheumatoid-arthritis-leaflet.

8 Moroni 10:22.

9 Mark 1:40

saying, "I will; be thou clean."[10] The parable is inspiring . . . and distressing. I hold three separate statements as truth: God can do miracles. God loves me and is moved with compassion for me too. I will deal with increasing pain and disability for the rest of my life. For me and for many others who pray for healing, Christ apparently says, "I will not." I know He can; that fills me with hope. But for some reason, He chooses not to; that is difficult.

* * *

A few years ago when Sister Davis, the Relief Society president, learned that another medication had gone wrong for me, she cornered me at church.

Sitting on a metal folding chair in the back of a classroom, she tugged her shirt and crossed her legs right over left, then left over right. "How can we help you?" she asked, looking uncomfortable but concerned. In typical LDS fashion, she suggested that the Relief Society bring in meals.

I laughed. "That is so nice of you. It really is, but I am not getting well anytime soon. What are you going to do? Bring me dinner for the rest of my life?" I smiled and ran my fingers through my hair, pulling out more loose strands, then laughed again to let her know I was joking.

She didn't laugh or flinch. Her eyes were clear and tearless, and her voice was steady. "If we need to."

I blinked. She'd caught me in the little "I'm fine" lie I told everyone every day.

Apparently I became the topic of a meeting because Sister Marshall called the next morning. "I am bringing you dinner tonight. You can't tell me no. I'll be by at five thirty," and she hung up the phone. For the next five nights, my family ate casseroles and fruit salads, cookies and cakes, breads and vegetables—more food than even five hungry children can eat. I begged the women to stop so we could eat leftovers and not have food go to waste, insisting again that I was fine and meaning it for once. A small miracle.

* * *

Sometimes it seems as if my life is like a moonless night, dark and dim, obscure and shadowy; I am easily overwhelmed by the gloom. But a few bright stars stud the crushed-velvet sky, even on the darkest of nights. I wait for starry flashes and firmly direct myself to notice them: I am sitting on

---

10 Mark 1:41.

the couch and realize I am not in pain. It is shocking and short-lived, but I relish it—a good day, I declare, for that moment alone. My little girl puts on one of her ninja/princess outfits, complete with purple satin cape and metallic green head scarf. She dances through the kitchen, points her finger at me, and announces, "Guess who I love?" I smile at her crooked grin and twinkling eyes, and I see her as she is meant to be seen. The minililacs by the front sidewalk bloom—late, like always, because the north-facing planter never receives full sun. The shady coolness makes growing anything but moss difficult, but it is also a rare gift: while other lilacs have wilted and faded grayish-blue, mine are fresh and violet, fully blooming and fragrant for Mother's Day. It is a small thing, but I breathe in deeply, the lightly perfumed air floating around me. My sister brings dinner, not because I am particularly worse today but simply because she lives next door and she likes cooking because she can, and she likes serving, and she does. I savor her spices and her kindness, tasting her fiery jalapeños and love long after the dishes are washed and she has returned home.

When my life of necessity moves slowly, there is ample opportunity to live deeply in small moments. For that, I am grateful.

* * *

I used to live briskly and efficiently through big and small things—family, home, work, service, and play. I was useful to and needed by so many, and I liked it; being useful was good.

The question now is whether being chronically ill is good too. I know things now, and I know them in bone-deep, sink-to-the-marrow ways. There are things worse than having chronic illness; one of them is watching someone you love hurt when you can do nothing to help. People can love you even though you don't do anything for them. To ask for help when you know you will never repay the favor is humbling and liberating. Some of the most important lessons we should teach our children—things like compassion and service—are learned best when they discover someone is in genuine need. Perhaps suffering is my greatest gift to my children, the greatest lesson I will ever teach.

* * *

I wish I were brave enough to insist that what I have learned is well worth the pain, that I would not choose any other way. But that would be another lie. I would return to being healthy in a heartbeat, were it up to me. For years, I kept that little secret as if God didn't know, as if saying it meant I was faithless, as if it were sacrilege to question the hard things in life. I don't think that anymore. I think Christ knows how it feels to want "this cup [to] pass."[11] I think He understands not wanting to live through what lies ahead, and I don't think He is upset when I tell Him I'm afraid, that I don't want to do it, that I didn't know how hard it would be. He knows.

Why Heavenly Father thinks this is a good way for me to live is a mystery I may never solve. Here I am, ready to serve anyone with all my might, mind, and strength, yet I find myself encompassed about by worries, anger, weaknesses, swollen joints, and shaking limbs. I am not a vigorous instrument in His hands. My old life revolved around working hard and being busy and industrious. I see many people around me living that good life, that shoulder-to-the-wheel, anxiously engaged life. I have been given a different part, and my new life is slow and unproductive; things rarely get accomplished, and I have squarely set aside my old goals of getting PhDs, writing books, and harvesting big gardens. But I have time for the peaceable things. People and relationships and love—for them, I have time and ability.

* * *

The angel Gabriel told Mary, "With God nothing shall be impossible."[12] I used to imagine that Gabriel's "impossible" things were astonishing healings, dramatic environmental wonders, and spiritual marvels. To be healed would indeed be miraculous—black-and-white, intense, direct, grandiose, and marvelous; I revel in the possibility and pray daily for the mere chance. But there is another type of miracle, slow and hazy, so unhurried and obscure that I have to squint my spiritual eyes and search my soul to know if I see it at all. The misty miracle lingers in daily-ness, a sacrament cup filled one meager drop at a time, a soul sanctified by a slow redemptive burn, a chapter in the book of life written word by exquisitely painful word. I am starting to understand the power of a God and the suffering of a Savior who are with me moment by unbearable moment, hour upon painful hour, and day upon drawn-out day, bringing a semblance of grace and peace, illuminating a deep darkness. I see Their handiwork in the "chronic" help given me by godly friends, neighbors, and

---

11 Matthew 26:39.
12 Luke 1:37.

family around me. I thought people would get as tired of helping me as I am of feeling ill. They have not.

Healing my troubled body will take a miracle; anyone can see that. But enduring the next forty or so years is impossible. Utterly impossible. The years stretch out interminably, and I see the future, however much I try not to. I simply cannot do it. And yet, by the grace of God, I live day by day with two (or three) diseases, medication side effects, financial pressure, and burdened relationships—sometimes crying and whining and breaking down, sometimes denying and lying, sometimes losing my hair, always praying and pleading and searching. In that, God reveals the most majestic, most lasting, most impossible miracle I can imagine.

Through Him, nothing is impossible.

"Help thou mine unbelief."[13]

* * *

On good days and Sundays, I am hopeful. But Monday and another week of life with chronic illness comes too soon.

Being sick has changed things for me. For one, I have lost the fear of my own death. Pain, I fear; death, not so much. Hair is overrated, and no event—be it ever so fancy and formal—requires wearing uncomfortable shoes. People can be ruder than I ever imagined and more kind than I ever dreamed, sometimes at the same time. I can color on the sacrament meeting program or sing "Put Your Shoulder to the Wheel"—whichever I feel best about. Some blessed husbands are statistical outliers who will shave your armpits happily, and some children must chop vegetables while their friends are texting. Healthy denial is my favorite dysfunction, but breakdowns are lovely, and I am open to delusions and other psychotic behaviors. Many clichés about illness and faith are true, but that doesn't mean they are helpful or nice to say. Medication usage demands balancing side effects with the symptoms of a disease, and there is never an easy answer. I am not my illness, but my illness has changed who I am.

This is my reality, one filled with difficult, unrelenting adjustment. Some days my prayer is simple: *Help me care enough to get up and do this. Again.*

That I do is a miracle. Just another small, bittersweet, chronic miracle.

---

13 Mark 9:24–27.

3
Blindness: Seeing with a Disability
by Kris Belcher

I HAVE ALWAYS LOVED THE account in 3 Nephi where Christ visits the people in the Americas and invites them, one by one, to feel the wounds in His hands and feet. He teaches them, prays with and for them, and blesses their little children. My favorite part comes when Christ inquires, "Have ye any that are sick among you? Bring them hither. Have ye any that are lame, or blind, or halt, or maimed, or leprous, or that are withered, or that are deaf, or that are afflicted in any manner? Bring them hither and I will heal them, for I have compassion upon you."[14]

Oh, how I wish I could have been there! How wonderful it would have been to have been led to Jesus and to have felt His gentle kindness and power as He healed my sightless eyes.

I have had countless opportunities to plead for and received Christ's healing; however, that healing has not always come as I have desired.

All my life I have dealt with limited vision and eventual blindness. As an infant, I was diagnosed with bilateral retinoblastoma, or cancer in the retinas of both eyes. I was treated with radiation, which killed the cancer. Thankfully, the medical team saved my life and some vision in both eyes, yet as my facial bones grew, the area that had been treated with radiation did not, resulting in an hourglass-shaped face.

This malformation became increasingly difficult for me to handle as I grew older. I didn't want to be the one people stared at in public, but I was. I didn't want to be different from others, but physically, I was. I certainly didn't want to be the one people referred to as "disabled" or "handicapped" (words I loathe), but, again, I was. I wished I could have a beautiful and attractive face, but unfortunately, I could not.

---

14 3 Nephi 17:7.

During my dating years, my visual impairment and abnormal facial structure were catalysts for tremendous heartbreak. My many guy friends were just that—friends. I felt like the love counselor for every single male on the continent, but no one considered me as a possibility. I stopped counting the times I heard that I had everything, but they couldn't get past my eye problems.

I clung to the promises Father in Heaven had given to me regarding marriage and motherhood; however, I couldn't imagine how He would ever make them work out. Was there a man on earth who could really see me for who I was, really love me?

Well, it turned out there was. Following my mission to Louisville, Kentucky, I met James. He was the best friend of one of my missionary friends, and we hit it off right away. I didn't give dating him much thought, however, thinking he would end up like the others, afraid of getting too close to the girl with the disability.

But James was different. We started dating, and when we discussed all the physical problems I had, it didn't faze him. What? Was this guy for real?

I prayed to know if he was right for me to marry and received my answer in a priesthood blessing. I was told that James had been prepared for me. If I didn't choose to marry him, another would be provided, but James would make me happy. I did choose to marry him, and we began our life together.

After two indescribably difficult pregnancies, our children, Christopher and Benjamin, joined our family. Christopher and I almost didn't survive the pregnancy, and because it was so difficult, James and I knew it would take a heavenly manifestation to have another baby. Well, the manifestation came a few years later, and I endured another nine months of horrific illness.

When Benjamin was one, our lives turned upside down. At this point, I had only limited sight in my right eye, having lost the vision in my left eye when I was around nine years old. And now the thing I most dreaded seemed a possibility.

My worst nightmare became reality when my vision began to fade, and I learned there was cancer, caused by my childhood radiation, growing on my optic nerve. In order to save my life, my eye would have to be removed. Of course, this was not the news I wanted to hear. Complete devastation doesn't even begin to describe how I felt when I learned I would never see again.

As if this wasn't enough, on my way into surgery, the doctor explained that he would need to remove all the tissue, nerves, muscle, and some bone in my eye socket—anything that might have been exposed to the cancer. It would be impossible for me to have a normal artificial eye because I would not have a normal eye socket.

In absolute horror, I asked what I would do for an eye and was told I had two options: I could either wear a black patch or wear a pair of glasses with an eyeball attached.

Needless to say, I had no desire to be a pirate or Mrs. Potato Head and definitely required the sedation they administered. My horrible situation just kept getting worse and worse, and I was a wreck.

When I awoke from this surgery, I was completely distraught. The darkness not only enveloped my eyes but also crowded my mind and heart. I was blind and would never see again. Of course, I knew I would see again after death, but even that knowledge couldn't remove the immediate pain and deep sorrow I felt.

It was impossible to describe the severity of my emotions. I literally felt unwhole. It felt as though the surgeon had carved out a piece of my soul when he'd used the scalpel to remove my eye. It seemed strange. I was not my body, and yet something was definitely missing from my core.

I could barely stand to touch my wound site and was disgusted by what my own face had become. I couldn't understand how my husband could still love me. I didn't even love myself. I couldn't imagine how I would ever live in the dark with a huge hole in my head. What would I do? How would I ever go on?

Upon further investigation, I found out that a silicone facial prosthetic could be constructed that would adhere to my skin, and an artificial eye could sit inside of it. I was upset that this was as close as I could get to an eye, but it was sure better than the pirate idea or trick eyeball glasses.

After five surgeries in five months, the doctors believed they had removed all the cancer, but I didn't want to live, not blind and further disfigured. It took a long time to work through my feelings of loss, anger, sadness, and despair. I worked long and hard to recover physically, and I attended school for the blind in order to adapt to my world of darkness. Yet the feeling of being unwhole remained.

* * *

My journey back to health, both physically and emotionally, has literally been a moment-by-moment process. It has seemed as though I have continually cried to my Father in Heaven for strength, for comfort, and for healing, and though there has not been a miraculous cure, there has been healing. It has come a little at a time, with time. My body might not be whole, but I no longer feel incomplete inside my heart and spirit. Almost imperceptibly, Father has brought me through the darkness and despair to a place of confidence and strength.

* * *

Time, training, and trust in the Lord got me through that first year and a half. Gratefully, I cannot recall many of the specifics along my painful journey, but I can remember when I was finally ready to live again.

My family and I moved from our wonderful ward in Riverton, Utah, to another home in Lehi, Utah, in order to be closer to my husband's work. This made it possible for James to help me more. Being in a new place, in a new situation, was a fresh start for me. I was excited to be an active and positive participant in my own life, family, and ward.

Now I am able to live blind, something I never dreamed possible. I am able to smile again and even laugh at the embarrassing situations I find myself in due to my blindness. One summer, after an hour's drive, we arrived at our family reunion in a canyon near Salt Lake City, and I had one thing on my mind: I had to find the restroom.

Before we joined my husband's family around the campfire, we detoured into the cabin. I opened the bathroom door, then closed and locked it. I leaned my cane in the corner and got ready to sit on the toilet. However, as I was sitting down, I reached out my hand to find the toilet and instead felt a head of hair! Needless to say I yanked up my pants really fast.

Noting the altitude of the head, I deduced it was a young head and was probably a bit disturbed by what had flashed before its eyes. Talk about hindsight.

Trying to reassure my new friend, I inquired, "Was that scary?"

"Uh-huh."

It spoke! The head could speak! Why it hadn't found its voice earlier, I'm not sure, but I was glad to hear it, nonetheless. After apologizing, I left my bathroom buddy and walked out to the group, shaking my head in disbelief. When they saw me approach, the family asked what was wrong.

"I'll pay for therapy," I said. "Some little girl in the bathroom is going to need it."

* * *

Because I can now laugh about my situation, I am able to see that life is worth the struggle, and the struggle can turn me to Christ. By turning to Him, I can receive His strength to move forward. On those days when it's so hard to be blind, I let my sadness turn me to Father in prayer. I ask Him to give me the strength I lack, and He helps me through until I am strong again.

I still worry that I am stared at in public. I still don't have the face I wish I had and am still not able to do all the things I would like to do, but I am grateful for the power of grace that carries me through these difficulties.

One area in which I need Heavenly Father's help is communicating, especially with my husband. It's difficult not to be able to read body language visually. I can't see his reactions, his facial cues that would let me know he's happy, sad, worried, etc. So I have to listen for other clues. I can catch a lot by what he doesn't say or by the feeling exuded from his posture. James is a naturally happy man, so when he isn't goofing around or singing some show tune, it's a pretty good bet that something is on his mind.

I used to be able to see the love he has for me in his gorgeous hazel eyes; however, I can't do that anymore. So we both get to work on our verbal expression and patience with each other, and many times it actually works.

And since I have no movement in my eyes, I too am not able to express nonverbally all that I feel. It kind of takes out the punch when I have to say, "I'm rolling my eyes at you!" or "I'm glaring at you!"

For the most part, we do very well together. We're great friends, and Heavenly Father was right: James has made me very happy.

Then there are the kids. I'm often asked if my boys try to get away with things because I can't see what they're doing. Well, of course. What boy doesn't try to get away with more than his mother wants him to? But I know more than they think I do. I often have to remind them that I'm blind, not stupid.

For some time, one of my sons was stuck in the lovely preteen, anti-personal hygiene phase, and it was a constant battle to convince him that a shower was truly quite necessary. One particular day, he finally conceded and went into the bathroom and closed the door. I heard the water turn on and then the shower curtain slide into place. Now, it would appear he was getting the job done, but the water didn't sound right. It didn't sound like he was actually in the shower, so I opened the bathroom door, and there was my son—outside the shower—fully dressed.

"What?" he asked defensively.

"It might help if you got *in* the shower. You might actually get clean."

He had been caught, and he knew it. The suspicions I had harbored for several days had been proven correct. My darling son had been fake showering for who knows how long. Anytime I had asked if he had showered, he'd said, "Yes. Feel my hair."

His hair had always been wet, but he hadn't really showered. This smart boy had only been going through the motions to fool his mother, who didn't have the ability to see. Additionally, due to the severing of my olfactory nerve in an invasive surgery, I couldn't smell him either.

On another occasion, after being asked repeatedly to brush his teeth, my son again entered the bathroom. I heard him open the medicine cabinet, turn on the water in the sink, and make swishing noises with his mouth. After a while, he spit into the sink and tapped on its edge. What did he think? That I was stupid? I might not have been able to see and depended almost solely on my hearing, but come on.

"It'll work better if you use a toothbrush and actually put it in your mouth," I called.

"Oh man!" was the next sound I heard from the bathroom.

Caught again!

Although I'm blind, I still clean the house, do the laundry, help the boys with homework and, like others, have to figure out the answer to the eternal question of what's for dinner. It isn't always easy. There are many times I grow frustrated, and so do my children and husband. We have all had to adapt.

I try not to worry about the things I can't do and focus on what I can do. And one thing I can do is love my children better than anyone else can. Being a mother, blind or sighted, is a tough job, but I feel peace knowing that Heavenly Father is invested in my boys more than I am. He will help me become the mother He wants me to be.

During my trial with cancer, I did not receive a miraculous cure that would allow me to maintain my eyesight. Similarly, I was not spared

pain or deep sorrow, and because of this, I know I am being polished
and refined. I have experienced the healing and peace that comes
through the Atonement of Jesus Christ.

I, with Alma, know that "whosoever shall put their trust in God shall
be supported in their trials, and their troubles, and their afflictions, and
shall be lifted up at the last day."[15]

Not only can we be lifted up at the last day, but we can also be lifted
up each day as we place our trust in God. We can trust that he knows and
cares about our pain, struggles, and sorrows, and we can trust that he will
send his enabling power to help us through those things that are too hard
for us to bear.

* * *

You and I may not have been present when Christ healed the Nephite
people, but we can definitely experience His healing power.

I know that because of Christ's Atonement, all that is now unfair
and imperfect will be made right. Because of His Resurrection, I will
one day be made whole. I will live again with a perfected body and will
see through perfected eyes. It is this knowledge that sustains me through
each of my days in the dark.

---

15 Alma 36:3.

Part III: Financial

4

Financial Stressors: Will You Be Poor for Me?

by Andrea Palmer

CAN YOU PRETEND?

Let's pretend we are really good friends . . . Let's say we're sitting at the park and it's a beautiful summer day. Early summer. There is hardly any breeze. Our kids are playing and having a wonderful time.

Let's pretend we are good enough friends that we don't have to really say much to understand each other. You feel my heart. You know my energy. You understand that when I say something like, "I am doing fine," it's a lie.

Today is one of those days.

We hug, sit down together, exchange formalities. Our kids finish their snacks and head out to play. And then you look at me and say, "Andrea, how are you doing?"

"Oh, I'm doing pretty good," I say.

Then you call my bluff. "Really?"

I turn to you. I look at you. Then my shoulders slump, and I collapse into you, and then the sobbing starts.

Can I tell you my story? Will you really listen and hear me? Because today, I need it—and I have a feeling *you* need it too.

* * *

I was thirty years old when I got married in 2007. I had experienced much success in the professional world, and my husband was involved with a very successful asset management and investing group at the time. He was a managing partner and helped organize and set up a vacation club with the various assets involved with the group.

Needless to say, financial worries were not an issue for us. I actually often thought to myself, *I'm a little sad that we won't go through the "hard college years" together*. I remembered my mom and dad talking about how they had learned to depend on each other when they'd had to struggle financially to make it. Part of me actually felt like I was missing out because we were *never* going to go through that together.

It is funny looking back; I can see where these thoughts and feelings were almost preparing me for what was about to come in the next few years.

Slowly but surely, throughout 2008, our asset management accounts started tapering off. "Oh, it's just a phase," everyone in the office was saying. By fall 2008, when the market crashed, we knew the phase was going to be a lot longer than we'd expected.

Our clients lost homes, which meant we lost their business. We started losing our own investments—investments in oil, emeralds, property, mining projects, and other industries. We were in shock at how fast everything was depleted, how quickly everything around us disappeared. Literally overnight, we lost hundreds of thousands of dollars—as did so many others all over the country.

We kept trying to put more money into the business to somehow save it, but that money disappeared, and disappeared quickly. We'd had so much money and success that we just kept thinking, *There is no way we could lose everything*.

But we did.

* * *

I was pregnant with our first baby through 2008. As everything disintegrated around me, I had major doubts about whether or not we could take care of a family properly. The night before I had our Gabriel, I looked at Brent with eyes that must have said volumes. I didn't say anything aloud, but he knew.

He looked back at me, almost like a puppy trying to find approval, and said, "That is the first time you have ever looked at me and wondered if I could really take care of our family. . . . That's the first time I have ever seen you doubt me."

Looking back, I feel terrible for allowing that feeling into my heart. It must have been demoralizing for him.

* * *

When I say we lost everything, I really mean that—we lost *everything*: our money, our savings, our homes, our business. We went into debt to try to salvage anything within our business, but within months I was looking at my bank account and seeing that we had only twelve dollars to our name. Literally twelve dollars. And we had no idea how we were going to pay our gas bill the next day.

* * *

I remember getting a phone call from a collector. I told him I couldn't pay him. I started to cry.

"If you don't pay this bill this month," he said, "it is going to go to collections."

My only reply was, "Sir, if you were me, would you pay this bill or go buy diapers for your baby? Because I can only do one of them."

He was a very kind man. He paused and then said, "Ma'am, go get what you need for your child first."

Every bill we had went to collections. By this point, it was summer of 2009. We went day by day, not having any idea how we were going to get money to keep our lights on. My husband was working so hard to keep anything he could of our business; it was something he'd thought was going to sustain his family for the rest of his life. Additionally, he looked for jobs. I looked for jobs, but there were no jobs to be had. We were unemployed, penniless renters with no direction.

* * *

I ended up getting pregnant at the end of 2009, a complete surprise baby. When I found out, I sobbed. "How are we going to do this?"

I remember a very specific day when I was standing in the shower, sobbing because our utilities were going to be turned off the next day. I was completely overwhelmed by the thought of trying to take care of one more person.

But then our Natalia came to me.

She was suddenly just there—her spirit was right next to me. She, with a feeling of rejection, said, "Mom, you were so excited for Gabriel to come. . . . Why aren't you excited for me?"

It was like someone had stabbed me in the heart, and I was physically jolted. That was a turning point for me. Until then I had been in major denial. I'd been enveloped in anxiety and even depression about what was going on around me. But when Natalia came to me and talked to me like that, the Spirit shook me almost violently. It was like Heavenly Father was grabbing me by my shoulders and saying, "Andrea, wake up!

You can't allow this to take over your life!" It was almost like I had a flash forward twenty years down the road, and I was a bitter, poor, old woman constantly stressed out about just surviving . . . and I'd passed it on to my children.

That was something I would *not* allow. I had imagined my life so different from this—I would *not* allow that to happen. I was a mother of an amazing generation to come. I could not allow our financial failures to control my ultimate outlook on life.

Financial calamity taking over my life included a feeling of helplessness difficult to describe or explain, but I knew I had to be an agent who chose to act and not be acted upon.[16]

Months went by, and we struggled. We were both finally able to let go of the old business and start new business ventures, which was a challenge all its own. We looked for jobs; there wasn't much there. But we also had to admit that we were both too entrepreneurial to work for someone else. I had Natalia in July 2010. To make ends meet, my husband worked on the new business during the day and waited tables at night.

We were truly in our own "college of life." My wish had come true.

* * *

One Sunday, a member of our ward, Brother Smith,[17] stood up to bear his testimony and tell about his financial struggles. He was also an entrepreneur and had also lost his business. He was talking about how he was having such a hard time understanding why the Lord would allow him to go through this. He was a good father. He was faithful. He was following every commandment he could think of. He had received specific inspiration for his business. But it seemed like the windows of heaven had closed on him.

I remember listening to his testimony, and everything he was saying was exactly what I was feeling. Then he said he had decided to call our stake president to talk with him about it. They were good friends, and he needed his counsel. Brother Smith said he asked the stake president, "Was this all worth it? Why would I get so many answers to continue this business if we were just going to fail? I have failed. Why was this all just a big failure?"

Then the stake president immediately said with a stern, fatherly voice, "Brother Smith, what is the purpose of this life?"

---

16 See 2 Nephi 2:13–16.
17 Name changed for protection.

"To gain our exaltation and live with God."

"And how do we do that?"

To which Brother Smith recounted all the usual Primary answers. Then our wise president said, "Yes, but you are missing one element. We can only gain exaltation because of coming closer to Christ. Feeling Him. Loving Him. Begging Him for forgiveness and healing. Truly *knowing* Christ and allowing *Him* to save you. Now . . . has this experience taught you how to do all these things?"

Brother Smith paused, thinking solemnly, then answered, "Yes."

To which our president said, "Then I see no failure here."

When he shared that experience, my chest pounded. I had felt the same way. My thoughts had run that same course: *If we were directed and led to so many different business pursuits only to have them fail, then why did we do them in the first place? If we were told to try so many different things and they didn't work, why did we try? Why are we in a* worse *place after following the Lord's counsel?*

I bowed my head, and tears welled in my eyes as I sat there on the bench. I knew the truth was in the answer "Then I see no failure here." Everything we had experienced up to that point *had* brought us closer to the arms of our Savior.

* * *

After losing our business, looking for jobs, then trying more businesses and projects, both Brent and I were worn down. We had gotten used to the stress of trying to figure out how to pay our bills, and in a way, we had gotten into a groove of dealing with the constant stress of survival literally day by day.

It was easy to start to assume that life *should* be a struggle. It was an interesting balance of learning how to endure well but not allowing myself to subconsciously look for hardships and, therefore, cocreate it energetically. At this point, we had to start looking for abundance instead of scarcity, which is why I believe Heavenly Father gave me this tender mercy on this particular day.

I put my kids down to take a nap, and then I went into my room and collapsed onto my knees. I prayed so hard. I knelt and wept and sobbed . . . and wept and sobbed some more. I was so tired. I was so exhausted. I was ready to be done with this lesson.

After not feeling very much while kneeling down, I moved and sat down next to the door in my bedroom, where I could see out the window;

I just sat there looking outside and started having another conversation with Heavenly Father. "Father, I will do anything you want me to do. I am willing to do *anything* to help us get past this point in our lives. I am willing to do *anything* you ask of me . . . willing to sacrifice *anything* you ask of me. I am willing to—"

Then the Spirit interrupted me. That didn't happen often because He was a good listener, but He literally *interrupted* me.

"Andrea, would you be poor for me? Are you willing to be where you are for me *right now* and stay here for the rest of your life if this is what I want for you?"

I swallowed—and it felt like I had a lump of coal in my throat. My immediate answer was not a resounding yes. I fought it instead. I thought, *But why would you want me to have this constant stress in my life?*

To which He said, "Would you be willing to stay exactly where you are for the rest of your life for me?"

"But this isn't what you want for me! You don't want me to stay like this for the rest of my life!"

"But *are you willing* to do this, experience everything you are feeling *immediately*, right now, for me?"

I couldn't respond. *Would I be willing to do this for the Lord forever if that is what He wants me to do?* It had never crossed my mind that perhaps what I was experiencing every day *was* my sacrifice. It was my anything.

Needless to say, I did not give Him an immediate yes. I had to pray for it. The willingness to do *anything* for the Lord, even to go through my immediate everyday circumstances willingly, to accept it as His will for me with *joy,* knowing it might not ever change . . . that kind of willingness came after days and days of prayer . . . and asking for forgiveness because I wasn't humble enough to say yes immediately. I had to learn how to consecrate everything, every trial that came every day in order to be humble enough to say yes immediately to anything the Lord asked me to do.

* * *

Reflecting on my change of heart after my daughter's visit, I faced some decisions about my everyday life as far as our financial situation went. Money had always been a weak point for me, a responsibility I'd always shrugged off; it was easy to take money for granted, not remembering that every penny was the Lord's and had to be accounted for—every penny spent and every penny earned. There were some things I had never really faced before this particular trial, the most prominent of which was that the world around us viewed and valued us by our money. By the abundance of it or lack thereof, money was like air in our world; if anyone suddenly didn't have it, they were breathless and panicked, grasping at anything that would keep them from dying. But miraculously, like air, I learned that we shouldn't worry so much about where money was going to come from because it was something that would flow to us through the mercy of Heavenly Father. He provided it all, and it was all His. I learned these lessons, like so many others, from studying the scriptures, particularly the words of King Benjamin.[18]

I had to decide every day to see myself as God saw me, to value myself as He did. I could choose to be a victim or choose to be in charge of my life. I could choose constant despair, or I could choose faith. I could choose to try to control everything around me hopelessly alone or choose Christ's Atonement and healing to govern the situation.

I decided I was going to focus spiritually on every situation and see Christ in it. I was blessed spiritually in each situation, such as when my kids screamed, my house was messy, a bill collector called, ants crawled in my kitchen, another rejection letter came, we couldn't pay our power bill, or a friend called to go shopping. Everything that happened to us, day in and day out, was an obstacle placed in our path to see how we were going to handle it. And I can personally testify that when I used those obstacles for my spiritual growth instead of allowing panic, fear, frustration, and anger to overcome me, the Lord came to help, and help abundantly. It made me realize how ungrateful I had become. I decided to use all of my experiences to focus on Christ instead of on the frustrations and failures and to become grateful again.

When a bill collector called, I would say, "Thank you, Father, because I have a phone to take calls from." Or when our car would break down or a child would spill milk all over the floor, I would say, "Thank you, Father, because I can use this stress to grow spiritually." When I would read a bill we couldn't pay, I would say, "Thank you for giving me eyes to see this." Or when my kids were screaming, I would say, "Thank you for giving me children who are alive and have energy enough to scream." I started saying, "Thank you" for everything—*everything*. What I focused on expanded without fail. If I focused on the lack of anything, I got more lack and saw more lack. When I focused on gratitude, I always got

---

18 Mosiah 2–5.

more and saw more to be grateful for.[19] All of this served as a reminder to keep praying and keep giving thanks to Heavenly Father for everything I had. These enticements drew me closer to my Savior. They helped me remember the suffering He experienced in the Atonement for me.

It was amazing when I started doing this to realize how much I had given in to the thoughts and whisperings of Satan. I realized how easily I was frustrated with my kids and how I blamed my frustration on financial stress. I blamed pretty much everything around me on finances. My husband and I had allowed negative words to permeate our vocabulary, like "We can't" and "There is no way" and "It's not possible." In this way, we were allowing our situation to feed upon itself. Because we were creating lack of abundance mentally, we were also allowing ourselves to create a perspective of the world that was full of want and scarcity.

* * *

I understand now why so many marriages fail because of financial stress. Inside of financial struggles, it is easy to blame the other person for the failure.

For me, that has been Satan's number-one strategy. I have been shocked at how many times, even out of the blue, I have been fed a thought from Satan that sounds something like, "Well, if Brent would just work harder he would be more successful." Or "Brent needs to get his focus right to get out of this pattern." Or "If Brent would take this more seriously and handle it, we wouldn't be in this mess." There are some thoughts I've been fed about him that I will never share. I have been rocked to my core, and it has floored me to see how much I have been attacked where our marriage is concerned. Satan finds every nook and cranny with any weakness and uses it to his advantage. I believe gratitude is the protection. The magnitude of what being grateful for everything truly means—especially about my husband and our eternal marriage—has been my defense.

There was one night, early in this whole situation, that I particularly remember, when we hadn't really talked or connected for a couple of weeks. We were both on edge as we looked at our checkbook. Brent was looking at the floor. I said something like, "Well, we have to figure this out," and my voice carried the accusation I felt. It caused Brent to shut down even more, which made me even more frustrated. I sat there looking

---

19 See Thomas S. Monson, "The Divine Gift of Gratitude," *Ensign*, Nov. 2010.

at him as he looked at his hands or the floor or the ceiling . . . anything to avoid the shame that making eye contact with me would bring to his heart.

Then something changed, and my Heavenly Father gave me a supreme gift—it was like all of a sudden I left my body and was looking down on us from above. I could see my energy and how Brent was retreating because of it. I was able to see him how God saw him: a man, a mighty, spiritual giant, a strong provider, an extremely talented soul, and then I started to cry. Here was a man who loved me so much, and he had no idea he was going to be put in such a position that he couldn't provide for his family. He was trying very hard to make things right. He was doing the best he knew how and wasn't getting any credit from me at all. All he felt from me was blame, anger, frustration, stress, and anxiety.

As I came back from my view above, I said I was sorry. I touched him, and I cried with him. We knew if we continued this pattern in our marriage, we wouldn't make it. And *nothing* was worth that to us. Nothing was worth losing our eternal family. We were willing to do anything to make sure our sealing promises stayed with us and our family forever.

* * *

There are several tools we've implemented to save ourselves and our relationship from the destruction and erosion of financial stress. We were able to build on the habits we had already formed together because we knew how vitally important it was to build an incredible root system so when the storms came our tree would be strong amidst the winds.

Instead of going to the temple once a month, we went once a week. We connected every night. We prayed out loud for each other during our couple prayers and expressed how much we loved each other and were so grateful for each other. We faithfully read our scriptures together. We promised each other we'd be "out of the box" and see each other how God saw us. We made the decision to love each other and touch each other as often as possible. I also made the personal decision that every time Brent walked in the door, I would immediately think of five reasons for why I was so in love with him, then I would give him a really good kiss.

Marriages don't fail because of finances. Marriages fail because people give in to the number-one attack from Satan—the attack on their spouse— and that can destroy even the strongest of marriages.

* * *

If you were to ask me about the most important spiritual lesson I have learned throughout the last few years, I would immediately reply, "Stewardship."

It is easy to say that everything is the Lord's with our mouths. It is much harder to actively live as if everything *is* the Lord's . . . including our debts and failures. Christ made everything—everything that was created and everything still being created, including the opportunity for us to go through our debt and financial difficulties.

When I finally learned to look at my debt and bills and say, "This is thine, Lord. What would you have me do?" the answers started flowing. I have ownership over nothing. Everything I have is the Lord's. We are told that in our temple endowment. Everything, including anything that might not be pretty. When we are willing to let go of our pride and give everything to Him, including the things we are ashamed of, He can take it and make it into something spectacular.

That is part of the miracle of the Atonement; it takes everything and makes it beautiful. Especially our trials. When Nephi was tied to the mast for three days, he praised God despite it all. That is why the compass worked for him, because of the attitude he maintained.

I like to think that my days can be similar to Nephi's. There have been many days when my home has been rocked to and fro, when I've felt like I am tied to the mast and being blown about in the wind. Nephi's days didn't get better when he was tied to the mast; in fact, until the end, his days got progressively worse—watching his wife cry, his children live in fear, his parents draw closer to death . . . yet amidst all of it, he stayed focused on the Savior.

We don't know if the Spirit testified to him that it was only going to be a three-or-four-day thing and then it would all be over. For all we know, Nephi thought they were all going to die. That is the question we must ask ourselves: how do I stay steady, praising my God, while not knowing how long this trial will last? And then we need to find a way to do it.

When I allow myself to give everything to the Lord and truly give Him all my failures as well and praise Him for it, that is when I am free to have power to work my personal Liahona. I am not perfect at it, but every day I get better, and progression is what matters.

* * *

Now, looking back on everything, I can see immediately how much the Lord kept blessing us. The day after I realized we had only twelve dollars to our name and we had to pay the gas bill, one of Brent's friends called and asked him to do some work on his home. Another time when we didn't know how we were going to pay rent, I received some work from connections I had and got an advance to pay the rent. We have always eaten and stayed healthy. Just having food on our table has been more than many of God's children have had in various areas of the world.

Miracles like that happened over and over again. I am sorry to say that for the first few months of it all, I never saw any of it as a miracle. I wish I had written more of it in my journal, but I was too focused on how stressed out we were about everything. When I made the choice to be grateful about everything, I finally saw how the Lord was taking care of us. Matthew 6:28, 30 took on a whole new meaning for me: "And why take ye thought for raiment? Consider the lilies of the field, how they grow; they toil not, neither do they spin. . . . Wherefore, if God so clothe the grass of the field, which to day is, and to morrow is cast into the oven, shall he not much more clothe you, O ye of little faith?"

My scripture study changed—it was like I was on a mission again. When I served in Russia, I searched and searched the scriptures for answers to everything. I had gotten out of that habit. Suddenly I was searching again. I was pondering spiritual things all the time again. The Lord was moving Brent and me toward another mission—understanding our life's purpose and what we must be prepared to give to the world. Through this whole experience, I have been blessed with great knowledge and wisdom.

I know that everything we have gone through for three-plus years has been a miracle for me, for Brent, and for our family. We have been blessed immensely in the last few months, and the miracles just keep coming! But I believe part of it is because I have finally allowed the Atonement to open my eyes to see it all with a humble heart and to be truly grateful for everything—the bad along with the good. It takes practice, but it is, oh, so worth it.

We will go through much more in our lives. We will face many more adversities. But my Savior will carry me the entire way, and that is where my peace comes from. I feel Him next to me. I see Him when I pray. I see my children's eyes light up when they know He is in our home, blessing us. It was perfect timing for me to become a mother of young children while going through this. Children are happy, even when they have nothing.

Learning how to have a child's heart and submit to the Lord like they do is an amazing experience. Godly happiness can happen in the midst of constant stress and adversity. Having the joy of a child is more than being happy; it is the key to having charity.[20]

* * *

These are some of the most important lessons I have learned through all of this:

—My value and worth are not defined by money, not by how much I have or by how much I don't have.

—Never, never, never allow myself to play the blame game with Brent. There is no excuse to treat my spouse badly. Ever. There is no excuse to allow stress to overtake my emotions. Every day I have the choice to be happy. I have the choice to take hold of my life and love it no matter what is going on around me.

—Reading, praying, and meditating are everyday habits for me. I have made myself make time for them no matter what. I make the choice to create peace for myself through those things.

—I am a much better steward over everything physical in my life right now. I am full of gratitude for everything I have. There were many months where I had to learn this gratitude. But I did. No matter what, we have shelter, food, and clothing. The Lord has given us healthy children. There are so many things to be grateful for.

—I have taught myself to look at each day through a spiritual lens— to live in every moment and allow myself to feel everything instead of burying it inside.

—I am self-reliant, and making it in this world is not about my resources; it is about my resourcefulness. The Lord has helped me have new eyes for how to take care of the things I want and need without money. I have traded a lot and have done everything I can (especially because I am not working) to make my home beautiful with pennies. I have learned how to get a new wardrobe with only ten dollars, how to make meals cheaply, how to effectively grocery shop, and how to find new toys for under three dollars for my kids. I can say no to nonessential things.

---

20 See Moroni 7:45–48.

—I am immensely grateful that the Church was willing to help us when we needed it. What a blessing it is to have the Church's short-term support.

* * *

Now that we are friends, we can tell the truth about ourselves. We can open the door to greater faith and lessen the isolation by sharing the real-life struggles that come to us all.

I prayed for the gift to love my life no matter what was going on around me, and I have been given that gift. I will not lie; it is a lot of work, but I cannot tell you enough how amazingly He gives back. The first day I started to focus spiritually on everything, the Lord gave me so much peace I was overwhelmed. He will always do the same for you.

Love your adversities. Love them. Because there is no failure if it brings you closer to Christ.

5
Life after Depression, Divorce, and Bankruptcy

by Barbara Matthews

I COME FROM A LINEAGE with just the right amount of sacrilege and sacrifice to allow for good storytelling—stories of divorce, poverty, and adultery that have been buried under enough generations of Church attendance, community service, and strong work ethic that, by the time I was born, they had become just that—stories.

I grew up going to Primary, Young Women activities, family reunions, and temple dedications. My family of eight often knelt in a circle and prayed together, squeezing hands before letting go at amen. It was a childhood of gospel-oriented action, and even though I'd heard my ancestors' stories, youthful invincibility and innocence made me feel impervious to similar heartaches. I held hard work and even harder prayer in such high esteem that I felt my actions could forge the life I wanted.

* * *

When I was about twenty-one, I experienced for the first time that raging, fear-induced anxiety that accompanies the sudden awareness that no matter how much I prayed or how hard I worked, I couldn't force the outcome I desired. I had entered a dating dry spell, and all I wanted was to get married and have babies. But without a boyfriend, I (in my mind) was fast approaching old-maid territory with no way to avoid it. I knew mine was a righteous desire, but I also knew righteous desires weren't always granted. Though I prayed and flirted, not one single boy showed a speck of interest. I was frantically impatient at times, writing dire sentences in my journal about how God's will and my own perceived lack of physical beauty were conspiring against me.

Then, after nearly three years of yearning for a husband, I fell in love. Six months later, we were married. The emptiness and fear were washed away by wholeness and clarity of direction—new feelings in my yet young life.

I remember one of those perfect, dusky nights when my husband and I sat on the small patch of grass outside our house-converted-to-apartments home, holding our tiny daughter and looking up at the few stars whose brightness outshone the city lights. I felt such a completeness of love and protection and peace. All was well. I'd accomplished the goals of my youth—college, temple marriage, motherhood. From here on out, as far as I was concerned, we'd be growing a family, growing our bank account, and growing our marriage. We'd eventually join this daughter in the temple for her own marriage, serve senior missions, and fill our lives with the richness of grandchildren who would bring laughter and youthfulness into the quietness of old age. It was a beautiful picture I'd dreamed, although naïve.

For a time—nearly eight years to be exact—life moved forward in the way I had pictured it. Oh, don't misunderstand. There were what I considered small challenges: pregnancies slow to come, financial setbacks, and imperfect personality traits I had to tame into more Christlike attributes. But I was blissfully happy, content to be married to a man I desperately loved and glad to build a career while saving for the time when my husband would finish school and I would come home to my gloriously blonde babies.

* * *

Loss comes into everyone's life. Like nearly everyone I knew, I experienced it: the boyfriend who chose someone else, the grandparent who passed to the other side of the veil, the friend whose life ended long before the years showed on his face. But in the early stages of my life and marriage, I knew nothing of the character-altering type of loss that can be required on our path heavenward: the giving away of those things most precious, of losing one's life for Christ's sake.[21] But I was about to get a crash course. Within a three-year span, I would lose my mental health, my financial stability, and my marriage.

Let me take a step back and give you the historical view. In January 2005, I set a New Year's resolution not unlike others I'd set in the past. I was going to spend more time doing the little things that are really the big things in the gospel: studying the scriptures, praying with my family, praying on my own. I had let the ever-mounting pressures in my life—

---

21 See Matthew 10:39.

callings, work, laundry, potty training—get in the way of my connection with my Father. I wanted to get back to that place where I was praying at all times and in all things.

It was a time of nourishing and fertilizing my roots. My resolution didn't fade with the days of January like most resolutions did. Instead, daily study of the gospel became increasingly important and desirable. I know now that God cleared my schedule, that the expanding power of the Atonement increased my desire for spiritual things, that I was being prepared for the deep pruning that would take place.

I was pregnant with my third child and was still working full time, saving every possible cent so I could quit my job once the baby arrived. My husband had graduated from college and had gone back to work, and though his income was much smaller than mine, I thought that if I had a small nest egg and gave it time, we would figure out how to live on less. In April, I gave birth to Joshua and became a stay-at-home mom. What I didn't expect was the crippling postpartum depression that came along with my beautiful son.

Two months later, as I was fighting my way through mind-numbing darkness, a friend approached me to see if I was interested in helping found a magazine for women in Utah. *Wasatch Woman Magazine* quickly became my passion, giving me something to focus on and easing—although not erasing—the loneliness and lack of direction I felt. I threw myself wholeheartedly into creating a publication that would bring women together by celebrating both their differences and their similarities.

Just as we prepared for the publication of our first issue, my husband confessed to an ongoing, long-term problem with pornography. As the facts of his indulgences were revealed over the following months, I learned of his general dissatisfaction in the life I'd found so fulfilling. But I was undeterred. I knew that with God's help and with hard work, we could put back together the marriage I thought we already had. Unfortunately, I'd forgotten the lesson from my youth: no amount of my work or the strength of my desire could change the outcome of another person's choices. Just like in my twenties when I couldn't make an object of my affection fall in love with me and propose marriage, I now couldn't make my husband do the work that would heal him and help him overcome his addiction.

We spent the next two years in ever-increasing turmoil. We saw therapists and bishops and friends who had "been there." I read self-help book after self-help book, summarizing the suggestions to him at night when I would hold him close and hope to regain his heart.

The ugly truth was that I blamed myself. I thought I wasn't pretty enough or that I had been too critical, too demanding. When he asked to quit his job so he could help with the magazine, I acquiesced. I wanted to support him in any way I could.

Without his income, it was only a few months before we couldn't pay the bills. I returned to work, my heart heavy at the thought of leaving the babies I'd finally come home to. I juggled two full-time jobs, one that paid and one—the magazine—that I clung to stubbornly despite the ever-piling debt. I prayed and fasted and went to the temple. I placed all my hope in miracles.

But the miracles I wanted—a loyal and repentant husband and funding for the magazine—didn't come. In late 2007, I realized my income no longer covered the payments that needed to be made to keep the magazine viable. I prayed for guidance, and the answer, quiet and peaceful, was to sell the magazine and declare bankruptcy. It was a Nephi-slaying-Laban moment for me. Bankruptcy felt dishonest, devastating, embarrassing, and evil. Through my prayers, I'd felt I was doing God's will by keeping the magazine alive. This answer of bankruptcy made me doubt my ability to hear my Father, to recognize His guidance. But through continued prayer, I came to accept that bankruptcy was indeed the answer. At the same time, my husband's cycle from "let's work on things" to "let's call it quits" grew ever shorter. One night, when I confronted him with another falsehood I'd uncovered, I told him the marriage was over. The confirmation that came from the Spirit filled my entire body—it was the loudest silence I'd ever heard.

* * *

The final giving away of my life happened fairly quickly. We sold the magazine, filed for bankruptcy, and then filed for divorce within a matter of three months. There was an intense feeling of failure in it all—that my hard work and my striving for righteousness had not been enough to keep the life I'd been given. But in my quieter, heart-open moments, I recognized that I had given up what I wanted for the future God had planned.

The years after were a time of healing and regrowth. I remember the exhaustion shortly after the divorce; it was so deep I couldn't endure the social interaction that came with ward socials and Relief Society events. It left me staring blankly at my computer screen during work hours and sent me home to collapse on the couch, surrounded by crayons and unfinished homework and leftover fast food. I remember the undulations of numbness followed by pain, pain that escaped through screams when I was surrounded by the privacy of my car with the radio turned up too loudly. But I also remember the way I was carried and cared for during those first intense months. The ministering of angels came in unexpected ways. I felt my grandmother's presence, her arms holding me when the loss felt excruciating. And one dark evening, when I prayed for relief, unseen hands were placed on my head, and I was given peace to sleep through the night.

This ministering, though, was not solely performed by those beyond the veil. My friends and family kept me busy and nourished with food and words of comfort. My employers promoted me despite my many unproductive hours so I could afford an in-home nanny. And my children knelt with me in prayer, holding hands and squeezing at amen.

Days turned into months, and I eventually fell in love again. I remarried, gained a stepson, and gave birth to a daughter. I studied and prayed and found answers to the exhaustion and the depression. Little by little, my health returned, and my heart lightened.

* * *

The truth is that at times I mourn the lost innocence, the fearless way I used to attack life, yet I can't begrudge my God. He has given me faith in place of innocence. When I look around at the life I have now, surrounded by five children—a combination of his, mine, and ours—I can see God's plan unfolding. I crawl into bed at night next to a man I trust completely, who I know is faithful to me and to our children but most importantly to our Savior. Together, we are growing, striving for the eternity we both want.

I see the compensatory blessings I've been given in place of the role of stay-at-home mother.

My Father has lightened the financial burden I carry and has opened the way for me to have more time with my children. I have been given opportunities to work from home so I can be around for the goings and comings. I sometimes get to fulfill the roles of taxi driver, nurse, and short-order cook. I can again imagine a future with children who live the gospel and bring their babies home to visit me.

Mostly, though, I see a life that is God-directed rather than self-directed. I am being reshaped, remolded, and regrown. My story now mingles with those of my ancestors. It tells of some loss and some sin, but it also tells of the enabling and healing power of the Atonement, of the beauty of mortal life, and of the love of a Father in Heaven who blesses His children.

Part IV: Family

6
Choosing Charity When Children Choose a Different Path
by Alice Ann Weber

MOTHERHOOD BEGAN FOR ME LONG before my first baby was born. I longed for it from the time I was a little girl. I tended the children in every home on our street. I adored my nephews and nieces. To become a mother was my cherished dream. My first baby came fourteen months after I was married.

I was in awe at the miracle of birth, that golden, ethereal moment when a grown spirit comes to earth in a tiny, mortal body. I devoted all my soul, energy, and motherly love to caring for that first little one. I wrote down every move and milestone in his baby book. And that same wonderment continued with the seven babies who followed. I had always wanted and planned for a big family—eight children was my dream! My ability to love expanded and grew as my family grew. I knew God had blessed me richly with healthy, beautiful children.

As our wonderful family sat on the bench at church, all eight children dressed and shined, I'm sure everyone thought we were the perfect Mormon family. I thought so myself. We did all the things a good Mormon family should. In fact, one of our neighbors in his mission farewell talked about coming over to our home every morning, sometimes getting a taste of our big healthy breakfast, and then kneeling in family prayer before he and my son took off to school. We seldom missed sending our children off with a prayer in the morning, and we seldom missed a united family prayer before bed. Sometimes our family nights were sliding contests across the kitchen floor with a teething baby screaming in our ears, but our intent was there.

Those were crazy years of dance, piano, violin, and harp lessons, as well as Cub Scouts, football, basketball, science projects, and Church activities. We traveled, snowmobiled, and boated—there were so many fun and happy times together.

Often when attending the temple, I dreamed of the time I would be able to bring my children there. What kind of temple dress would each of the girls prefer? I wondered. When I saw girls who resembled my own five daughters, it was exhilarating. Dreams would swirl in my head of the happy times when our family would gather for the beautiful temple weddings of my daughters (and, of course, my sons). When I would watch brides pose for a photo in front of the temple, I could hardly wait until it was my own daughter in that picture.

* * *

Well, my life had a mind of its own, and so did my children!

One day my little girl came home from Primary and said, "No one is going to tell me where I'm getting married! I don't have to get married in the temple if I don't want to." I was stunned and speechless. From that point on, I consciously tried to be gentle and persuasive without being controlling. I wanted to lead in love and wanted to respect my children's agency, hoping that our testimonies and active devotion to the Lord would show them the way.

As the years quickly sped by, I sat with that same little girl as we read the Book of Mormon together so she could go on the river trip with the youth in the ward. I tried so hard to give her my testimony. I struggled to get her to Beehive camp. That same beautiful girl, as a Mia Maid, wouldn't go to class, even though I was her instructor. When she was a Laurel, she found her belongings on the front porch when she came home from Lake Powell. She had taken off with a boyfriend, and I was so angry and disappointed. I didn't know what to do!

Slowly, over the years, my expectations began to crumble. I assumed my children would all grow up loving our Savior, cherishing the truths of the Book of Mormon, developing strong testimonies of the Restoration of The Church of Jesus Christ of Latter-day Saints, and marrying in the temple, but life doesn't always turn out as we think it should. It's a crushing blow when that happens. Children don't always make the choices we would like them to.

* * *

My life totally fell apart when my daughter (on scholarship at BYU) became pregnant and then, shortly thereafter, another daughter married a man from Morocco who was Muslim. My heart ached when my son decided against a mission. I cried when one daughter, who had just received her Young Women medallion a couple of years previously, moved in with her boyfriend, and when my youngest daughter checked out of seminary (the first one out of the eight who didn't graduate). It seemed the perfect Mormon family was falling apart. I had a throbbing pain inside. How could I survive?

I had a hard time joining in conversations, hearing talks or lessons, or keeping on with normal life because each of those somehow reminded me of my disappointments. Someone always mentioned temple weddings or missions or children who were following the gospel plan. I'm ashamed to say I avoided friends because it was too difficult to hear about their children's seemingly perfect lives. I became isolated in my sorrow, feeling sure I was a complete and total failure in the thing I had most longed for: being a good mother.

It would be difficult to have one child go astray, but to have several of my children making decisions that led them in pathways outside of Church activity was devastating. The hurt was unbearable, and with added financial and marital instability, I felt the darkness of despair. I was numb, wondering how I could keep going. Sometimes when I tried to pray, words wouldn't come. At those times, I would sing a hymn because I knew the song of the heart was as good as a prayer. The hymns were a great source of peace, as was the temple.

* * *

The scriptures had always blessed my life, but I now found they had even greater meaning. Moroni 7:45 was the beginning of my healing. It taught me how the Savior wanted me to move forward. It was a blueprint I wanted to follow. "And charity suffereth long, and is kind, and envieth not, and is not puffed up, seeketh not her own, is not easily provoked, thinketh no evil, and rejoiceth not in iniquity but rejoiceth in the truth, beareth all things, believeth all things, hopeth all things, endureth all things."

It taught me how the Savior wanted me to go forward. I learned, using this scripture as a model, to be tolerant and respectful, forcing myself to bite my tongue when I wanted to say something that wouldn't foster good feelings. I continually reminded myself to think positive, uplifting things about my children. If my thoughts were negative about them, it seemed like it would always pop out in unkind words or a judgmental attitude. I realized I could disagree with their actions while maintaining my love for them. A follower of Christ would think no evil, especially of her own children, and would love her kids unconditionally—no matter what.

Charity really was the answer. I read this scripture often. I had to be patient and trust in the Lord's timetable with my children. I had to develop great faith, knowing He knew the big picture. Besides being patient with my children, I had to be patient with myself and my imperfections because I was a work in process. I didn't have to be perfect to be an example. I focused on showing my kids the joy of service in the Church and living God's plan of happiness. I had to keep full of faith and hope, which I found usually came to me with time in the scriptures and fervent prayer.

I also had to nurture my own needs—to eat carefully, get my rest, and constantly learn and grow. Walking in the beautiful world God created always lifted my spirits when I was down. So did making bread and sharing it with others. (My children's friends loved coming over to eat the whole wheat "Mormon bread.") Any act of service gave me great joy.

I learned to be grateful. It helped me get through disappointment and grief. Instead of mourning what I didn't have, I learned to appreciate what I did have and build on that. It was so important to focus on the positive!

When I was full of gratitude, I didn't envy others; I only felt blessed. Yet, when I yielded to jealousy and pride, I couldn't talk to others or be happy for them in their successes with their children. I was more worried about my self-image than about my children. I had to realize my self-worth wasn't tied to my children being model LDS kids. I was a beloved and treasured daughter of God—always, no matter what.

Now, to show my children and grandchildren how much I love them, I listen much more than I talk, always showing interest in what they are doing. They are my top priority. We plan outings and fun times together. We talk on the phone, send e-mails, and text each other. Whenever they invite me somewhere or need me, if at all possible, I am there! I cherish every minute I can be with my precious family. Charity is the pure love of Christ. Focus on that love!

* * *

My husband and I contemplated what we could do to strengthen our family. We needed to bring unity and cohesiveness to both our adult children and the three who were still living at home. We needed to have a vision of where we were heading, so we invited everyone to help formulate a mission statement, a declaration of what was important to us. Some children participated more than others, but it was a group effort.

WEBER FAMILY MISSION STATEMENT
We are Compassionate & Kind
A Motivated Family
Showing Respect and Commitment
We Are FOREVER FRIENDS

As this mission statement hung (at times) on the walls of each family, it was a compass that directed our pathways. I've been impressed with how it has directed the kind of people we've become. It really describes our family, and we have, subconsciously perhaps, let it guide us through the years.

Here I need to stop for a moment and celebrate the wonderful family I have.

We are compassionate and kind. It's wonderful to see our children support each other in times of need. There have been several instances in which compassion and kindness have made a difference with family members. In financial issues, siblings have sent money to help, such as with a hospital procedure or visit, the sale of a home that was upside down and money was needed at the closing, buying a car someone needed to sell, paying for car repairs, sending money to help someone finish college, and giving a piano to another family. It's wonderful to see our children support each other in times of need.

We are a motivated family. Each of our children has graduated from college, and some have master's degrees. They are hard workers, and all have great careers. They are also very active in sports, coaching their children's teams and participating in marathons, triathlons, and twenty-four-hour relay races, both in biking and running. This qualifies for a motivated family! Two sons-in-law, who are especially close friends, climbed to the top of the Grand Teton together.

We show respect and commitment. Learning tolerance and respect for my Islamic son-in-law has been a great opportunity. Through him, I realized how close-minded I had been to anything I didn't know about or understand. We had the wonderful opportunity of having my daughter and her new husband live with us after they were married.

I respected the goodness of this new son of mine. We listened, intrigued, as he told about his devoted parents and the life he'd lived in Morocco.

He was open and communicative. It was amazing to learn how many similarities existed between the Muslims and Mormons; in fact, that was something that drew our daughter to him. At the present, their two daughters study Islam and the Arabic language once a week and are learning good things. Our daughter supports her husband's devotion to his family's beliefs and remains respectful of ours. Our family has been respectful and kind to each other. It's a comfortable situation, and we all enjoy being together.

We are forever friends. Recently, when our granddaughter was married in the temple, everyone in our family was there to support her. They gathered from Boston, Seattle, Idaho, and Utah—thirty-eight of us: eight children with their spouses and nineteen grandchildren. We had such a great time laughing and catching up on everything at the Sundance lodge we stayed at after the reception. We even get together at Bear Lake every other summer for a reunion with extended family. I'm always delighted to see them travel to see each other and enjoy being together as best friends.

And my five darling daughters are my closest friends. We text or talk every few days, and I'm so grateful for each of them and the wonderful women they have become. My sons are great men and have wonderful wives too.

* * *

I had a sweet experience that has helped me trust God and know that perhaps all situations in my life have some kind of purpose I can't comprehend right now with my limited understanding. I have to keep reminding myself I really did hear this because I wasn't even thinking about my family when the voice came into my mind. It was clear enough, though, that I remember it fully. The Spirit whispered to me, "I've handpicked your sons-in-law!"

That inspiration has made it easier to trust in God and not my own understanding. None of my daughters has married in the temple (well, not yet, anyway); however, I count my blessings every day because of the really great men they married. Although these men are not members of the Church, they are very good men!

To know that God is mindful of my children, their spouses, and my grandchildren with as much and more love than I have is such a blessing, such a comfort. After all, they are all His children too.

My kids used to say, "Mom, you have such great kids. Why are you so sad?"

They're right. I do have amazing children and grandchildren, and I am so thankful for all of them. My sorrow now comes not from the fact that they are not model LDS children but from the desire I have for them to come to know the Savior so He can help them through their burdens and so the power of the Atonement can empower them and enrich their lives.

* * *

I think this labor of raising children is hard work! We are carrying enormous loads. And the guilt and heaviness of heart when we think we have failed in our role as parents can be more than we can bear. When we learn to give our guilt, worry, and grieving to God and come unto Him, our load becomes light. We have given our heavy burdens to Christ in order to feel peace and joy. We must remember that when we are feeling heavy, it is time again to shift the load.

When I heard the following quote from Elder Holland about mothers, it really helped me lighten my load. I felt as if a great weight was gone from me. I received assurance that I wasn't carrying the whole weight alone in this difficult role of motherhood. All I needed to do was *ask* for His help:

"When you have come to the Lord in meekness and lowliness of heart and, as one mother said, "pounded on the doors of heaven to ask for, to plead for, to demand guidance and wisdom and help for this wondrous task" [of motherhood], that door is thrown open to provide you the influence and the help of all eternity. Claim the promises of the Savior of the world. Ask for the healing balm of the Atonement for whatever may be troubling you or your children. Know that in faith things will be made right in spite of you, or more correctly, because of you."

Elder Holland also said, "You can't possibly do this alone, but you *do* have help. The Master of Heaven and Earth is there to bless you—He who resolutely goes after the lost sheep, sweeps thoroughly to find the lost coin, waits everlastingly for the return of the prodigal son. Yours is the work of salvation, and therefore you will be magnified, compensated, made more than you are and better than you have ever been as you try to make honest effort, however feeble you may sometimes feel that to be."[22]

* * *

My Father has given me comfort and great joy. He has answered my prayers and heartfelt desires, and I'm sure He knows me by name and loves me.

---

22 "Because She Is a Mother," *Ensign*, May 1997.

He knows that through the years we have done the best we've known how. Our intent was to be perfect parents, and though we made mistakes, we somehow always made it through the rough times and saw miracles when the Lord provided for us. We always had a lovely home and food to eat. We can't go back and redo the past, but we can clear away the effects it's had on us. It is not productive to dwell on what we should have done or how we could have been better parents.

I found I could only go forward freely when I forsook the past. Writing an inventory of the past was like itemizing the junk cluttering my garage and then cleaning it out and throwing unneeded items away. It gave me more space for what I really needed in my life. In place of all the guilt, self-pity, pride, and self-righteousness, there was room to put what mattered most—my Savior Jesus Christ. I found I could give away all my sins, sorrows, and past mistakes and accept His great saving sacrifice for me. I could put Him in the center place in my heart and life.

We are so fortunate to have the weekly sacrament, which serves this same purpose. We can review the past week, gather our mistakes, repent, and then go on fresh and clean. I want to be more diligent in contemplating my past weaknesses and turning them into strengths. Each week I want to hear the Spirit's direction. I want to pledge myself to do His will.

* * *

I can't change the past; I can't change others, but I change myself. I can't force or control my children, but I can pray for them, love them, and never give up on them. I *can* regulate my own life so I can be eligible for exaltation and eternal life with my Father. Because of the wonderful blessings of the temple, I know I will have my children again. I know there is a strong binding link in place that will pull them back to us. Through our Savior Jesus Christ and His great Atonement, *all* things are possible. He will make all things right.

There are only two things my husband and I can do now. The first is to make sure we align ourselves with our Savior. We can follow the pattern He gave us of personal sanctification. He was obedient to the will of His Father. He always demonstrated great charity, especially in the Garden of Gethsemane and through His Atonement, and we too can love God and trust Him and His timetable. We can offer Him our broken hearts and contrite spirits. We can humbly yield our hearts to Him and receive the mighty spiritual power that comes to disciples of Christ who bear

His witness and stand strong and immovable. As we always remember Him and honor our covenants, He will empower us. We can do all things through Christ, who strengthens us.[23]

Finally, we can continue to have a positive influence in our children's and grandchildren's lives. We can constantly keep involved in their lives and show our interest and love. They need to know how much we care, how extremely precious they are to us and to their Heavenly Father.

We have to remember that when we share our testimonies, often just by showing them our commitment to our Savior and joyfully serving Him, it allows the Holy Ghost to remind them of the truths of their childhood. I've also been impressed to share the stories of our faithful ancestors and how their lives are living witnesses of their testimonies, devotion, and sacrifice to come to Zion and embrace the restored gospel of Jesus Christ with all of their hearts.

I know Heavenly Father loves my children—even more than I do. He will never forsake me. He will never forsake them. Just as Alma prayed for his wandering son, if I ask my Father to encircle my children with His great redeeming love, I know He will and that they will be in the best of hands.

---

23 See Philippians 4:13.

7
Death of a Baby: The Miracle and Memory of Little Madilyn

by Heather Jenson Hodge

IN AUGUST 2004, MY PATERNAL grandfather passed away. While attending his funeral, my husband, Brandon, and I received some very unexpected spiritual revelation regarding our future family. Three distinct, specific impressions came to both of us separately during the same talk at the funeral: one, we would have five children come into our family; two, there would be three girls and two boys; and three, the two boys would be at the end. It was an overwhelming experience as we shared our impressions with each other and realized we'd received them at the same time and in the exact same order. We knew we had truly been given heavenly direction.

As I had just given birth to our second daughter, Brianne, two weeks earlier, future family planning was the last thing on my mind. Pregnancy was not easy for me, to say the least. I have what's called an incompetent cervix. It is a condition in which the woman's cervix opens prematurely without any pain, usually resulting in the early birth of her baby—oftentimes, too early for the baby to survive. Treatment for this problem requires a risky surgical procedure known as a cerclage. Basically, the cervix is carefully sewn shut for added strength, which hopefully allows the woman to carry her baby nearly full-term. Most women lose their first baby before this condition is ever discovered.

When I was twenty weeks along with my first daughter, we went in for a routine appointment and ultrasound. What a sweet and precious moment it was to see our baby for the first time and hear that every little part was working properly. At the end of our appointment, as though it was an afterthought, the ultrasound tech decided to do a more thorough check of my cervix. Because of her diligence, she caught my cervical incompetence in time. Shortly thereafter, I headed to the University of Utah Hospital for surgery. As I was prepped for the procedure, it was determined that I was already dilated three centimeters, and the doctor could see our little Lauren's feet in the birth canal. Fortunately, everything worked out wonderfully with the surgery, and we welcomed our firstborn baby girl in July 2002. We were so thankful we had been spared the tragedy of losing a baby before finding out about my problem. We had been tremendously blessed.

After my grandfather's funeral, I felt relief in knowing what was required of me as a mother. The daunting question of how we would know when we were done having children had simply and spiritually been given to us. Five precious souls were coming into our home, and we looked forward with faith and joy to the journey that lay before us. We loved our two little girls and anticipated welcoming a third daughter sometime in the future.

* * *

A year passed by quickly. Life was busy with Brandon as a full-time student and full-time employee and both of us serving in Church callings that required extra hours out of the home each week. I enjoyed being a stay-at-home mom and found fulfillment in the challenge of entertaining two little ones all day long.

And then we found out I was expecting again and was due in July 2006. Life was going to get even more exciting!

When I was thirteen weeks along, the doctor determined that I needed a permanent cerclage stitched in my cervix to help keep this baby inside. With the placement and removal of two prior cerclages, I had permanent damage and scarring to my tissue. A permanent cerclage seemed like the best option for us to have a successful outcome, so we scheduled the surgery, and everything worked out well.

Two months later, we were at our ultrasound appointment awaiting the news that another girl was coming into our home, but we were shocked to find out that our daughter was actually a little boy! I felt puzzled and perplexed. I wasn't disappointed about carrying a healthy baby boy; it was just that this outcome was not in line with the prompting we had received months prior at the funeral. The revelation had come with such force—it was as if we had been hit by a spiritual bolt of lightning. Both Brandon and I knew the last of three crystal-clear impressions was that two boys would come at the end of our family.

Sadly, I began to doubt myself and these impressions. Maybe I wasn't as spiritually in-tune as I had thought I was. Why the mixed messages and contradictory outcome? It was a thought that quietly entered my mind every now and then for the remainder of my pregnancy.

After a smooth C-section delivery, we welcomed our first baby boy into the family and added another birthday in July. (Kind of crazy how all three of our children were born in the same month.) Lincoln's two older siblings adored and doted over him, and we soon realized we needed more space for our growing family. It was then that we made plans for our new home in North Salt Lake and anticipated the adventure that lay ahead in this new chapter of our lives.

* * *

Life was practically perfect. In February 2007, our little family of five moved into our newly built, quaint, corner-lot home in North Salt Lake. We were thrilled to begin a new chapter in our lives, and I was overjoyed to own my own four walls, have an enclosed garage to park in, and use two gray garbage cans all by myself that came with a personal pickup-and-dump service every Friday morning. It was great meeting new neighbors, fostering friendships, and planning playdates for our children. We reveled in the responsibilities of home ownership and felt proud of reaching this stage in our lives. I was in heaven. What more could a girl ask for?

The following month, I got my answer when we received a huge surprise: we had a fourth child coming to join our family in November. We were grateful and prepared ourselves to raise four kids under the age of five.

Lincoln was just seven months old at the time, and we knew life was going to get really interesting quickly around the Hodge home. Lincoln and this new little baby would be just sixteen months apart. At least it wasn't another July birthday, right?

Things progressed well with the pregnancy. At the conclusion of my first trimester, I was pleased with not having to go through another surgical procedure like I had with my three prior pregnancies because the permanent cerclage was already in place from the last baby. Daily life continued to get busier with three small children at home, and I had just been called as the Primary president in our newly formed ward. It was a huge undertaking getting all of the teachers called, manuals pulled together, and classrooms coordinated. Life was tiring but good.

In June, we received an exciting phone call. Dear friends from our previous neighborhood informed us they had some great news. The Schroaders had struggled with infertility for years and had recently made the decision to adopt in order to grow their family. They had called us to let us know that they had been chosen as parents for a set of premature twins. One boy and one girl. They were thrilled, and we couldn't have been happier for them.

She invited me to come visit them in the NICU at LDS Hospital and see their precious babies. I anxiously accepted her invitation, and one week later I was on my way to the hospital. I felt excited and nervous. I had never been in a NICU before, and I didn't know what to expect or how I would feel observing infants who weighed less than four pounds. Was I prepared to see the web of tubes and monitoring machines attached to these feeble frames, assisting them in sustaining life?

Before entering the NICU, I was required to meticulously wash and scrub my arms up to my elbows to eliminate any germs that could contaminate the room. As I was doing so, I smiled softly through the window as I saw my friend cuddling one of her newborns. I pushed open the door and slowly soaked in the sea of baby bassinets that lay in rows around the room. I made my way over to my dear friend and was overcome with emotion as I beheld her tiny twins and the gigantic grin on her face. She was so grateful to be a mother. Her babies were beautiful and were thriving quite well compared to many others in the room.

I remember being fixated on a father and mother who were a few steps away from me. They carefully caressed their small son of barely two pounds. I had never seen a baby that little before. I thought, *I could never handle this kind of situation. How are they doing this?* I stood in awe of the faithful families around me. I felt humbled by the healthy babies I got to take home from the hospital. Some families had been there for weeks, hoping and praying for miracles of healing for their little ones. It was a treasured teaching experience for me, and I would learn very soon that it meant more to me than I could have ever imagined.

* * *

July 2007 came, and it was a thrill celebrating our three children's birthdays. Lauren turned five, Brianne turned three (or thirteen—we couldn't tell which), and little Lincoln was a busy one-year-old. I could hardly believe how fast time had flown, and I was in total denial that my oldest daughter would start kindergarten the next month. We had just found out that baby number four was a girl, and everything looked great. I still had a hard time trying to wrap my head around what it was going to be like raising four little rascals ages five and under. Needless to say, I was thankful for my bountiful blessings and basked in the beauty and wonder of young motherhood.

Monday, July 30, was a morning I will never forget. Just after 6:00 a.m., Brandon's alarm went off to wake him up for work. Of course, because I'm a light sleeper, it always awoke me as well. As he was getting ready to go, I decided to roll over to get out of bed and start my morning by making breakfast for the family. As soon as both feet hit the floor, I felt fluid running down my legs. *Oh my goodness, I just peed myself*, I thought. *Oh, the joys of pregnancy!* As I made my way to the bathroom, I soon realized there was a real problem. I knew my water had broken, and I began to panic because I was only twenty-one weeks along—far too early for a baby to be born. Fear struck my heart as I told Brandon what was happening. We called my mom for help, and a sweet neighbor friend came over to be with our kids until my mom arrived. Then we immediately left for LDS Hospital.

Upon our arrival, I was rushed into a delivery room, where several tests confirmed that my water had indeed broken. I tried to be brave as reality started to sink in, but I couldn't contain the stream of tears that slowly dripped down my face and disappeared into the pillow. The doctors gave us three scenarios of how our situation would most likely play out: one, my body would, within the hour, go into labor, and I would deliver the baby; two, I could sustain for two to three weeks before my body would begin the labor process; or three, in some circumstances there was an equal chance of actually making it full-term and having a successful delivery.

Only time would tell. What we did know was that I wasn't going back home. If I wanted to give my baby a fighting chance, I had to lie flat on my back all day, with only brief bathroom visits and a five-minute shower every couple of days. I was wheeled to my new home in the hospital, where I would spend an undetermined amount of time away from my three other children and husband.

For the first time in my life, I felt I had no control over my body. There was nothing I could do to repair the rupture in the water bag; I was constantly passing fluid, and it was imperative that I be obedient and follow the doctor's orders.

I did, however, have two things in my power: prayer and the priesthood. Brandon gave me a beautiful blessing in which I felt peace and assurance that all things would work out as they were supposed to. I was told to have faith and hope in Heavenly Father's plan. I prayed mightily for a miracle and chose to cleave to the counsel given me. I asked for guardian angels to be with me and with my family at home.

Although the circumstances were unpleasant, I tried to focus on the positives of my current situation. I had plenty of peace and quiet, except for the constant checkups from the nurses and resident doctors. I had three meals prepared for me each day and no laundry to do. I had time to read, listen to music, and ponder my personal testimony. I learned to appreciate the sweet sounds of my children's voices as I visited with them over the phone. My room was filled with the fragrant flowers and beautiful blooms delivered by thoughtful friends and family members, which truly lifted my spirits. I kept the cards and letters that were sent close to my bed and decorated the drab hospital walls with priceless homemade pictures. I felt loved and supported.

I was grateful for each day that passed, but before long, each day started to feel a bit longer than the one before. Loneliness crept in from time to time, and I was so thankful for the random visits from familiar faces of the outside world. I started missing my normal family life and felt guilty about the grandmas having to step in to keep the family functioning. I knew they didn't mind, but I had never been in need of so much help before, and it certainly felt uncomfortable at times. It was all getting harder—not that I expected this process to be easy; it was just that I'd never known how difficult and challenging it would be on so many different levels. I was being stretched emotionally, physically, and spiritually all at the same time. But even with all of that, I tried my best to remain positive and faithful.

* * *

I had made it one full week. I was pleased with the progress and was glad to still be pregnant. That Monday morning, as I turned on the news, I learned of a terrible tragedy that had occurred. Six miners had been entombed by a catastrophic collapse at the Crandall Canyon coal mine. Rescuers made multiple attempts to save the men, and over the next few days I became fixated on the facts and updates of their situation. Sadly, three rescuers lost their lives in a courageous quest to find these men, and six others were seriously injured. Unfortunately, the rescue attempts were determined much too dangerous, and after ten days of searching, the efforts came to an end. The six miners were never found.

This sad situation gave me some pivotal perspective. Hard things happen to all of us. The families caught in this catastrophe captured my heart and took my focus away from my own obstacles. I prayed for them. I cried for them. I asked for tender mercies to attend them in their tragic loss. I knew dealing with difficulties and disappointments was part of the purpose of mortality. I pondered how we couldn't always control our circumstances but we could choose to be absorbed by the adversity we faced or be polished by the perils that persisted in putting us down. It was a blessing for me, amidst my own tender trial, to get outside of myself and care for complete strangers who were suffering. What a life lesson I learned at that time.

* * *

The Friday of my second week in the hospital was a hard day. During a routine checkup, I was notified my situation was not good. My fluid levels measured only one centimeter, while the average amount for a pregnant woman was fifteen to twenty. The doctor seemed almost cruel as she bluntly told me my situation was dismal. I felt discouraged and defeated. It required all my energy to hold back the wave of emotions that wanted to explode from my eyes as I was wheeled back into my room. I retreated to the bathroom, where I found refuge and released the heartache I was experiencing. I sobbed relentlessly. I knew I needed heavenly help to heal the hurt and fleeting faith I felt. I prayed profoundly that my baby would survive and that my body would sustain her long enough to give her a fighting chance.

The next few days were filled with much introspection. I had never felt this challenged to the core before. Did I *truly* believe what I had professed to believe all my life? Did I *really* trust in God and His eternal plan? Did I have enough faith to let go of what I wanted and accept the will of God no matter the outcome? As I pondered these questions, I humbly came to this conclusion: Yes. Yes, I *really* did believe in these things. I knew God was in control and that maybe He just needed to hear that from me: that I trusted in Him and His plan and *knew* it was true.

I prayed again. There, lying in my hospital bed, I offered the most sincere audible prayer I had ever prayed. I felt so strongly that I needed to verbally let God know I believed in Him and it was okay if my little girl needed to pass on to her heavenly home. I told Him I trusted in my temple covenants and knew that if Brandon and I could stay true to our promises, she would be ours forever. It was an overwhelming spiritual experience for me, and I felt pure peace and love from my Father in Heaven.

The following evening, Brandon came to see me. I counted on his consistent, daily drop-by visits. Occasionally he would even get clearance to take me out for a twenty-minute "date," in which he would wheel me down to the main floor of the hospital, get delicious shakes, and then go outside so I could soak in some sunshine. These moments were magical for me, and I treasured those twenty minutes more than anything. On this occasion, I shared my spiritual experience with him, and he tenderly listened and supported me. I told him I had felt different all day. Something seemed off with my body, and before he left, I told him I needed him to stay close to the phone in case something happened that night.

A few hours later, at 2:00 a.m., I was abruptly awakened by terrible pain. I immediately called Brandon to alert him that I was going into labor and he needed to rush to the hospital quickly.

Because of prior planning, we knew how we would proceed. I had chosen to have my permanent cerclage removed to deliver the baby vaginally rather than going through a transverse C-section, which would result in a vertical cut and possible complications because I was only twenty-four weeks along. This could possibly end my chances of ever having a successful pregnancy again, but I had three other children I had to take into consideration. I had to do what was best for the family as a whole.

I was taken into the delivery room, and everything happened so fast. The doctor was only able to remove half of the cerclage before I delivered, which resulted in a terrible tear in my cervix. My sweet little baby was immediately passed through a window to awaiting doctors in the NICU. I didn't even get to look at her, and I heard no cries. I told Brandon to go be with her while the doctors finished working on me. I didn't know what to expect or how I should feel. I just wanted to be with her.

A little while later, my mother came and got me. She slowly wheeled me into the NICU so I could see my baby. I wasn't scared because I had been there before. God had given me a preview just over a month earlier of this special and sacred place that sustained these precious souls. Brandon was there by her side, and I wept as I saw her tiny body for the first time. Our little Madilyn was perfect. She weighed only one pound ten ounces and was just over twelve inches long. Her features resembled those of her siblings. Even though every part of her was premature, everything was perfectly formed. She was our little girl.

* * *

Over the next several hours, the hospital staff performed multiple tests, and we received the reports. A gentle, kind doctor tenderly told us that sustaining Madilyn's life away from the machines was next to impossible. In fact, she was given only a 1 percent chance. Her lungs were too underdeveloped and delicate, and when the NICU doctors were trying to help her, a tube had ripped a hole in her lungs. It was hard to hear, but it was surprisingly an easier outcome to accept than if we'd been given a fifty-fifty chance. God didn't make us deal with a difficult decision. It was decided for us. We knew what had to be done.

The doctors disconnected Madilyn from all of her tubes except the oxygen. I was finally able to hold her for the first time. She had two donated homemade blankets wrapped around her, and in a quiet corner of the NICU, my parents and I gathered close as Brandon gave her a name and a blessing. It was a beautiful and treasured moment.

With the oxygen still attached, we were taken into a special room where family could gather to hold and meet our little Madilyn. Many of my siblings were there, and Brandon's mother and sister from Idaho were able to join us.

I nervously held her close as she was prepped to have her oxygen tube removed. I didn't want her to be in any pain, and I didn't want her body to react in a certain way that would make this process any more difficult. It was such a tender mercy how she lay there peacefully still and calm. The Spirit permeated the room. Those present reverently took their time to say good-bye to our little girl. Every so often the nurses would listen to her heart. The time of death would be determined when they could no longer detect a heartbeat. She gave us one precious hour before she sweetly and softly passed away in my arms. The seven short hours she had spent with us changed our lives forever.

Her funeral was five days later. She was dressed in a beautiful white gown the hospital had given us and was wrapped in a soft, white, knitted blanket and laid in her casket. Loved ones shared talks and testimonies of the truthfulness of the gospel, and we took comfort in knowing we would be with our sweet Madilyn again.

After the service, she was taken to the Farmington City Cemetery, where a special spot had been chosen for her burial. Beautifully, Brandon dedicated her grave, and we all blew her kisses one last time. It was a sad and sweet moment as we said our final good-byes, and I prayed for strength for my small family.

* * *

As I settled back into home life, some days were just tough. I battled guilt about what had happened and things I should have done differently. I learned that grief comes in layers and hits at unexpected times and places.

The most difficult moment for me was six days after her funeral. It was a Sunday, and I was in the kitchen getting dinner ready when I received a phone call. It was my brother calling to share the wonderful news of the birth of their healthy nine-pound-plus baby girl. I expressed my genuine congratulations and held it together while talking with him. Our conversation ended, and I immediately found myself sobbing over the sink into the fresh potato peels. The pain was still so new, and my heart hurt.

* * *

Time is a great healer, and it did get easier as the days and months passed. I had made the choice that any situation or circumstance that reminded me of Madilyn was a *good* thing. They kept her memory alive. I often pondered on the prompting Brandon and I had been given three years earlier. We knew there was one more member to join our family, but I wanted to give my body and mind enough time to heal. I didn't know how it was possible to successfully carry another child, but I knew I had been prompted to do so.

* * *

One year passed. We celebrated Madilyn's birthday with personal love notes written on brightly colored balloons. We sang "Happy Birthday" to her and sent them floating up to heaven. We enjoyed eating angel food cake for dessert and decorated her headstone with pinwheels and flowers. It felt good to celebrate her little life and to let her know her family loved her and looked forward to the day we could all be together again.

The following week, I had an appointment with a perinatologist. Dr. Jackson was a specialist for high-risk pregnancy patients, and I was definitely one of those. I explained my history and how I worried about the possibility of becoming pregnant again. He told me of a rare procedure called interuterine cerclage, where, at thirteen weeks gestation, I could have a specialized C-section-like surgery. The pregnant uterus would be pulled out of my body and reinforced by stitching the base of the uterus, above the cervix. It was extremely high risk. He performed this procedure only once or twice a year at best, but I felt this information was an answer to our prayers. We proceeded in faith because we knew there was one more baby to come into our home.

In October, we found out I was pregnant. Yes, I was due in July 2009! Another July baby. I just hoped to make it close to July and have a positive outcome with this pregnancy. We put our complete trust and confidence in what had been spiritually communicated to us years before, and I was thankful for every day that passed with no problems.

In January, I received the special surgery. Recovery was challenging, but I knew we had done the right thing. At the follow-up appointment, all looked well, and I greatly anticipated the ultrasound appointment where we would find out the sex of the baby. I tried to prepare myself to not be disappointed if it was a girl. I mean, I just wanted a healthy and full-term pregnancy this time, but I wouldn't feel complete without a second son in our family, and I knew I couldn't carry another child. My body had done about all it could do to get this far. I had to have faith.

The big day came. I was nervous and excited. I prayed for strength and comfort. Brandon sweetly caressed my hand as I lay on the examination table. The doctor began the ultrasound, and I was astonished at the first thing I saw: there, waving in the amniotic fluid, was a little boy part. It was as if he was saying, "Hello. Here I am. I told you I would come." I burst out in tears and exhaled loudly at the relief I felt. It was a cleansing cry. God had not asked me to do more than I could do. His promises were sure. As clear as day, I heard these words spoken to me at that moment: "I told you the two boys would come at the end. Everything has worked out as it should."

Any last bit of lingering guilt and grief I was holding on to was immediately washed away. What happened to Madilyn was part of the plan put in place long before I'd become pregnant with her. God had prepared me years before with key knowledge and information at my grandfather's funeral. I now understood. I had eyes to see and ears to hear. Lincoln's place in our family as our third child was not a mistake. I had just misunderstood. The two boys were at the end of our family here in mortality. Everything had fallen perfectly into place eternally.

On July 7, I delivered our last baby by C-section. Benjamin was born strong and healthy, and how grateful I was that he was here safe and sound. We had done it. Brandon and I felt a sense of completeness and wholeness. Our family was here in its entirety. We thanked God for leading us the whole way through that five-year process.

* * *

Through these many experiences, I learned some valuable lessons: God is in control. He is compassionate and cares about our concerns. He wants to communicate with us and give us guidance if we open our ears to the promptings of the Spirit. He hears our prayers. He answers our prayers, and He allows hard things to happen to us. That is how we learn and grow. It is how we become polished, refined, and more like His Son, Jesus Christ. What matters most is what we anchor ourselves to when the storms of life are upon us.

He is a tender teacher, and we are to trust in His timing and His ways, even if we don't understand all the answers. He will prepare us and provide all that we need to endure the trials of life. He supports and sustains us when we are weak and feel beaten down with discouragement. He loves us. He wants us to lean on gospel principles and feel safety and security in the eternal covenants we make in the temple.

We need to prepare and nourish our roots of faith and testimony now. We never know when a hardship or challenge may be just around the corner, and when difficulties come, there may not be time to decide and decipher what we believe. Prior preparation to know the truth and have a testimony will make all the difference in our times of trouble. No matter what our challenges may be, if we allow God to guide us and if we trust in Him, we will get through the toughest of trials. We truly can do hard things with God!

8

Infertility: He Did for Me What I Could Not Do for Myself

by Carrie Ann Oscarson Rhodes

TODD AND I HAD BEEN married for five years before we realized we were having problems getting pregnant. We weren't clueless; we were just busy—enjoying each other, enjoying our jobs, and enjoying our nieces and nephews. We were enjoying life! I was thrilled that my brothers and sisters and friends were getting married and having children. Their happiness was my happiness. I guess that was what made my experience with infertility somewhat atypical.

Mine is not necessarily a story about personal anguish or my wrestle before God (although there is some of that). My story is about how I learned to accept service.

* * *

I grew up in the Midwest and on the East Coast in a happy and typical large Mormon family. My mom and dad met at Brigham Young University and married before graduation. While my dad had MBA ambitions and my mom had dreams of becoming a graphic designer, they decided to have children right away. Mom dropped out of school, and Dad took a job in retail before graduate school to support his rapidly growing family. Graduate school was further delayed when Dad accepted the call to be a mission president when he was twenty-nine years old. When my parents left for the mission presidents' training seminar, they had four children, the youngest being just two weeks old.

Experiences like this created a strong family bond and family culture: it didn't matter where we lived as long as we were together, and we would serve where we were called. This attitude came in handy as, due to my dad's successful career in retail, we moved about every three years, and each time we moved into a new ward, the bishop would put my mom and dad to work in callings that often required a lot of time and effort. Serving others was a serious, if not overt, family value. Frankly, Mom and Dad didn't speak to us about their service; it was often from other people that we found out about the time they had spent, some generous offering, or how they had helped someone else.

* * *

I was a happy kid who grew up to be a happy adult. I'm sure I have had as much bad luck as anyone, but I can always see a silver lining. This seems incongruous with my serious cadre of social anxieties and periods of depression, but even in my darkest moments, like Annie, I know the sun will come out tomorrow. I know that by helping others I help myself. When I feel low, I find someone to serve, even if all I can do is my husband's laundry.

In fact, in the years before our more serious fertility issues, I was the go-to family member when someone needed help. I was the available aunt, the extra adult, the in-house babysitter. I really loved being able to help my siblings, particularly with their kids. There were middle-of-the-night hospital visits, where kids were dropped off at our house; countless hours of free child care; cousin parties that gave parents a date night; meals brought in when there was illness; craft projects for busy little hands; etc. I was worth my weight in gold. Being available and helpful felt good. Besides, I liked being busy.

* * *

In 2006, we began to seek answers about our inability to conceive, but after two years of tests, procedures, and an operation, we were told the medical diagnosis was "unexplained infertility." We had done everything within our power up until this point, and we felt that we were at a dead end.

We considered all of our options and were prayerfully seeking out the best solutions. Of course, I was struggling with questions in my mind and heart, but I felt that the Lord was pleased with the path we had taken thus far. Well-meaning friends and family members would occasionally press us for information: Had we considered this option or that option? Did we eat enough flax seed? Did we have a good acupuncturist? Was our bed oriented east to west?

We had tried traditional and holistic medicines, alternative therapies, artificial insemination, and one round of in vitro fertilization. It had cost us $12,000 just for the IVF alone, basically our entire liquid savings at that point, and nothing had been successful. We were so disappointed; the IVF had been our Hail Mary. We would have liked to have tried IVF again, but we couldn't do it without incurring considerable debt.

* * *

Even while we were struggling to get pregnant month after month, I never felt bitter, angry, or overly sensitive when others had success—except once. A girl I am acquainted with seems to lead a charmed life. She is a successful designer, she married the love of her life, she's beautiful, she has a substantial trust fund, and she is so charming and kind that it's impossible to hate her for all of it.

When she announced on her blog that she was expecting, I think I actually groaned out loud. I thought, *Of course!* Not my most graceful moment. It was the first time it was hard for me to see someone else where I wanted to be.

With little joy, I followed her baby showers and her decorating the baby's room. I felt jealous. This is hard to admit because being so petty goes against my nature, and unfortunately, I learned my lesson at her expense when she lost her baby girl during her sixth month of pregnancy. The baby was stillborn. I was devastated for her, and I honestly felt sorrow and the need to repent of my feelings toward her.

I'd had my own struggles, but no amount of my sadness at *not* conceiving could compare to the sadness she felt at her loss. I decided I would rather go a lifetime with no children than lose one like that. Even though some truly wonderful things have happened for this friend since (starting her own successful business, living in exotic locales, having a darling baby girl, and an equally darling boy), I still feel sadness for her loss and for my failure to maintain a positive attitude throughout my trial.

Soon thereafter, I had a phone conversation with my younger sister Sarah in which she pressed me harder than usual about what we had been doing since the IVF. She left me with the uncomfortable impression that she thought there was more we could be doing, but I had assured her we were doing everything within our power, particularly within our financial power.

Sarah decided to become our fertility savior. She created a website, a blog (www.babyrhodesbud.blogspot.com), a logo, and a PayPal account. She contacted friends and family far and wide and invited them, along with friends of friends, to donate to the Baby Rhodesbud fund. Many of these people set up websites and accounts to sell their crafts and hobbies, and the proceeds went into an account for us. Others simply sent us a check. Sarah felt that we deserved to have a baby and that if money was the only thing standing in our way, she would do everything in her power to remove that obstacle for us so we could explore the IVF procedure again.

It is so difficult to explain what it is like to be the recipient of this type of charity. I remember writing thank you notes to complete strangers and struggling to find the words to adequately thank them for helping us start a family, to create life. Todd and I felt so humbled by the outpouring of love and support. In my blog, I expressed my feelings:

> But my thoughts and feelings are never far from those who have made this round [of IVF] possible. It is so humbling to be the recipient of funds, time, energy, industry, and prayer. I am way more comfortable being on the other end, but I am so grateful . . . beyond words, song, art, dance, or any other form or expression. If I could stage a fireworks show for all of you, over the water, on a warm summer's evening, after a delicious BBQ dinner and chocolate cake . . . that would only begin to express it. I love you. I have needed you. Thank you for being there.

* * *

That year we hosted my family for Christmas Eve. As it came time to exchange gifts, Todd and I were surprised to be presented with the only gift of the evening. All of the nieces, nephews, and family siblings had decided to forgo giving and receiving presents from each other that year, and we were presented with envelopes from each family containing cards, drawings, checks, and cash. I still have one crumpled envelope with a few bills and some loose change that I still can't bring myself to open, let alone deposit. It is a reminder for me of that night and of that precious gift from one particular six-year-old niece. Our nieces and nephews served us in other ways as well: they fasted for us and prayed for us in each family and personal prayer. That Christmas will always be a touchstone experience for our family, one we will all remember and cherish.

In all, the Baby Rhodesbud fund raised over $25,000.

The pressure, then, for these expensive procedures to work was intense. We began the IVF process again and e-mailed our family and friends to ask them to pray for us and to let them know what was going to happen on what dates. This time, as a result of the hormones, I became very ill with a condition called ovarian hyperstimulation syndrome (OHSS), in which a woman's ovaries go into hyperdrive and enlarge, causing extreme pain and discomfort. We were not able to implant the fertilized eggs, and we had to freeze them instead.

* * *

Life continued to move forward whether we were ready or not. Sometimes it felt easy, and sometimes there were seasons of stress. The next few months were the stressful kind. We did two implantations using the frozen eggs; one round resulted in an ectopic pregnancy and the other in a nonfetal mass.

After miscarrying the mass, we found ourselves in our darkest hour. We were living in someone else's home while our new home was being completed, and we missed our creature comforts, not to mention we were dealing with all of this in the darkness of deep winter. Even our dog, Fiona, was depressed. It was almost comical how bad and pathetic things were. Todd and I did a lot of talking, praying, and soul-searching at this time. Shortly thereafter, this is what I wrote on the Baby Rhodesbud blog:

> Here comes the hard part for some people to digest: I am okay with not having kids. This doesn't mean that we will not continue to pursue options, pray, fast, seek, and ask, but I want people who care about me to know (and to accept) that children may not be part of our earthly path, and while that may be sad for some, I have had ten years to come to grips with it, and I am okay. I do feel sad that we don't have kids to share the fun things with: holidays and family traditions are *so* much more fun and more meaningful with children.
>
> I do feel really sad that Todd and I might grow old with no one to look after us or care for us or visit us. Our posterity ends here. But I have dealt with all of these scenarios and ramifications, and I can handle them—I have to. This is what my life is!

Coming through that time of darkness, I really felt okay. I felt at peace. I felt happy. I felt lucky. I felt blessed. I had so many great things going for me. I was healthy, I loved my husband and he loved me, we each came from wonderful families, I had great friends, I loved my job, and we lived in a beautiful home exactly where we wanted to be. We really had a lot going for us. So what more could I ask of my Heavenly Father?

* * *

Todd and I enjoyed the next year by *not* thinking or worrying about our infertility—it was a fertility vacation. I thought I had learned my lesson to accept help and service from others, although I felt sad that their sacrifices had not resulted in a typical happy ending.

We still had a little money left in the Baby Rhodesbud fund and had a little more from the sale of our home. After much thought and prayer, we decided to make one more sacrifice. We wanted to lay our material goods on the altar of life and show God that our desire for family was more important to us than worldly wealth.

This time we kept it a secret.

To make a very long story short, I had a wonderful pregnancy. I was not sick, I was not unreasonably tired, and I got to spend the entire summer in Connecticut with Todd, who was on a work assignment. I often hung out at the pool with a friend, and I visited friends and family up and down the East Coast all summer. It was a serious blessing, and there was no stress!

But God was not done teaching me a lesson about accepting service.

Even during the birth of our darling son, Oliver, I was the recipient of many acts of service and kindness. Oliver came very suddenly over a month early while Todd was in Singapore on a work assignment. My house was an especially filthy disaster that week, there was no sweet, welcoming nursery set up, and I didn't have anyone to take me to the hospital. When I called my dear friend, she dropped everything she was doing, calmly helped me make decisions, and cheerfully drove me to the hospital.

I was blessed by this friend again as she organized a cleaning party in my home so that when we came back from the hospital with our tiny baby, we could introduce him to paradise and beauty instead of filth and chaos. My sister Amy and my brother Chip hurried to the hospital to be by my side, and Amy stayed with me throughout the twenty-four-hour labor and delivery. She then ran to the airport to pick up my husband

and dropped him off to be with me, even managing to feed him a meal somewhere in transport.

What in the world would I have done without others' help and intervention? Again, how could I express my feelings of deep gratitude? The thought of those ladies cleaning my bathroom floor covered in amniotic fluid footprints sends shivers down my spine, and I am humbled by it.

* * *

I have often said Oliver does not belong to Todd and me; he belongs to everyone. It may take a village to raise a child, but in our case, it took a village to get a child here. I continue to search out the lessons God has taught me throughout this long journey. I was obviously oblivious to His guidance since He repeated the lesson of "you cannot do this alone; you cannot do this without me" over and over again. I can see so clearly now how this experience has taught me about the Atonement.

Though it is so much easier to be the one serving, it is sinful pride that stands in the way when we don't allow others to serve us. We are commanded to love and serve each other and to love and serve God. Service fosters love. We serve those we love, and we come to love those we serve. I need to remember things like, if it had been *my* sweet friend who had needed a ride to the hospital, I would not have hesitated because I love her! I would have cleaned all of my friends' houses because I love them! To know they did the same for me out of love is sweet and precious to me.

As I work through my hang-ups about people serving me, I think of the one act of service I can never repay. I think of the Savior and the Atonement. My continuous lessons in humility are preparing me to *further* accept my need for the Savior. His acting on our behalf defines our whole existence. The summation of our journey here on earth is dependent on how we make use of that service He provided.

Sarah did for me what I could not do for myself. Many doctors and technicians did for us what Todd and I could not do for ourselves. The Savior did for us what we cannot do for ourselves.

When we find ourselves in the greatest need, He is there to help and serve and love. Often, He will help us through the acts of others who are in tune with His promptings and counsel. And He asks in return that we love and serve Him and our fellow man.

9

Hearing Loss but Hearing His Voice
by Kate Cowan

"Hi, I'm Nancy. Sorry to bother you. I know you are busy, but I wanted to let you know your daughter didn't pass her hearing test. It is probably just fluid in her ears."

I glanced up at the end of the bed.

"What? What was that?"

The lactation nurse next to me continued to toss her instructions in a fluid Japanese accent. I was barely comprehending anything she said, and now someone was telling me something about a hearing test?

Nancy waved and smiled. "Don't worry; I'll talk to your husband."

John walked to the end of the bed, and I watched him talk to the nurse and gather another folder of papers and a few phone numbers. I sincerely hoped we could keep track of all these instructions.

The lactation specialist asked me another question about the nutritional content of breast milk, and when I didn't know the answer, she launched into a story about her granddaughter and her ability to read at such a young age.

At that point, the only thought I had was how my daughter would never learn to read if I couldn't learn to breastfeed her. The poor baby was already doomed.

* * *

A few weeks later, I wobbled into the hospital with my little girl in her infant carrier. Evie was so tiny, and her ten layers of clothes didn't seem to be doing enough to protect her from the January bite.

On the second floor of the hospital, a woman welcomed us. I unbuckled and unwrapped my baby, and we were taken into a dim room where several sensors were pasted to Evie's head and neck. She was tired, and staying still in my arms was about the last thing she wanted to do. She wiggled gently as I watched the computer flash colored numbers and lines.

"Okay, do you see that orange line?" A nurse pointed to a monitor with an orange wavy line that stood out as it peaked just below a thick green line.

"That line is supposed to reach this height to show your daughter is within a normal hearing range. As you can see, she is still below where she needs to be. We will have to make another appointment with an audiologist."

Clenching my jaw till we were safely in the car, I accepted the paperwork and a reminder card for another appointment with an audiologist across the street. Then I called John from the car, my throat tightening with fear and worry. He calmly listened as I told him about the test results. Then he said, "I know you're worried, Kate, and you need to know it is going to be okay. Kids fail these tests all the time. She might just need some tubes in her ears when she gets older, and that is not a big deal."

My mind began to wander, and I found myself going cold. It was like I had been doused with icy guilt. It must have been that rock concert I went to, right? I knew it had been too loud for my ears, and now my daughter had lost her hearing because I'd been selfish and attended a concert. Or maybe it was because I never drank enough water when I was pregnant. Could that be it?

"But what if she really does have hearing loss?" I blurted. "What if I did something to make this happen?"

"If she has hearing loss," he said in an even voice, "we will be fine. We can handle this."

I wanted to believe him, but a consistent fear nagged at me. How could I communicate with my daughter if she couldn't hear me? My dad was legally blind, and watching his struggle had been hard. However, to me, the thought of not being able to hear a person's voice and connect with them verbally seemed like a literal hell. How would Evie know me if she couldn't recognize my voice? I thought of my life and how music had been so influential. What if I couldn't share this major part of myself with her? I thought of what it would have been like if I'd grown up without my hearing. Without music, I would have turned out to be a very different person. The thought scared me, and the possibility that my daughter might have been born without her hearing caused my whole body to ache.

As a child, I loved listening to music and singing in Primary. I was drawn to beautiful minor keys, meaningful words, and the layered delight of a song whose music and lyrics fit together like intricate strands of embroidery. Unfortunately, I quit piano lessons soon after I started.

By the time I was in junior high, I wasn't involved in much of anything except spending time with friends. My self-esteem was low. I had put on a lot of weight and not found a place where I fit in. I knew I loved music, but I was too afraid to participate in it since I had quit piano and felt miles behind other kids. My mom encouraged me to take a sophomore choir class in high school. It was then that I reconnected with my love of singing and made some long-lasting friends who are still with me to this day. My husband was one of those friends.

I sang my way through high school, received a vocal scholarship, and minored in music at Weber State University. I spent the better part of my college education in voice lessons, master classes, and choir performances. To me, singing was as vital as breathing. It allowed me to find self-esteem, and I found the courage to lose the extra weight and start taking care of my body. I sang to lift others in times of need during Church services, programs, and funerals. Singing was my way to reconnect with God, and it had become part of my identity. I couldn't think of a better way to share myself with my little girl.

During the pregnancy, I had read about the unborn baby's ability to hear inside the womb. Determined that she hear as much as possible as soon as possible, I'd attended all sorts of musical concerts whenever I could. My husband and I had sung the *Messiah* in a large community chorus. I'd read poems and stories to my tummy while I felt her long, fluid movements. But had she heard any of it?

* * *

A week later, we went for a *very* long test, with more probes and cords attached to my wiggling baby and more ranges, numbers, and, ultimately, more inconclusive data. It wasn't until three weeks later that Evie slept peacefully through the test at Primary Children's Hospital. It was that day, March 2, that the audiologists asked to leave the room and conference with each other before telling us the results of the tests. That wasn't a good sign.

A few moments later, the audiologists came back in.

"Our tests show her ears are clear of fluid and that her eardrum is reacting normally. We believe the loss is probably in the cochlea. This is called a sensorineural loss. There are tiny hairs that, once they are damaged or compromised, are irreplaceable. Therefore, her hearing loss is permanent."

"I'm sorry. What? Did you say my daughter will never recover her hearing?"

"Yes. From the test results today, it shows us that your daughter has permanent hearing loss."

My husband quickly spoke up. "How much can she hear? Because we have seen her startle at loud sounds, and we know she is not totally deaf. She *can* hear."

"We are not sure yet, but we think she has moderate loss, which means she can hear some things, but for her to be able to learn to speak properly, she will have to be fitted for hearing aids."

While the audiologists tried to give us information about Evie getting fitted for hearing-aid ear molds, the word *permanent* rolled around in my head like a piece of bad fruit. How did they know from a couple of probes and a computer that my daughter wouldn't hear well for the rest of her life?

I let them talk while my mind spun. I felt numb, yet part of me was certain it must be a mistake. Everything was supposed to be fine with the first child. I had demonstrated faith by having Evie, and I knew it would be a miracle to get her here healthy and well. And now my worst fear had happened. She hadn't arrived perfect and whole. I began to cry out of sheer disbelief.

We were told that since Evie's birth was not premature and since nothing serious had happened during the pregnancy, it had to be a genetic problem. But they warned us that we might never find out what the true cause of her loss was.

One of the audiologists reached over and patted my hand, fresh tears in her eyes. I could tell this was hard for her and that this one time she had let her guard down and compassionately grieved with me.

As we left, Evie whimpered for a bottle and then smiled broadly, as was her latest habit. She looked at us with a grin and seemed to be gently reminding us that life needed to go on and we needed to get her some lunch.

* * *

That night while I cried in my husband's arms, he told me a story about a man and his horse. The man loved his horse and would give anything for it. But one day the horse fell down a well. The man grabbed as many people as he could to help get the horse out, but nothing he tried worked. The horse was stuck and would die soon. In despair, the man gathered the townspeople, and they decided to shovel dirt into the well to bury the horse. As they shoveled dirt in, it fell on the horse's back. The horse shook the dirt off his back and took a step up. More dirt was shoveled in, and the horse again shook it off and stepped up. Step after step, the horse got higher. Soon it was able to clamber up and out of the well.

My husband smiled and said, "When we get dirt thrown on our backs, we can choose to lie down and get buried, or we can step up."

On the same note, my grandma repeatedly told me I come from a long line of strong women. I knew Evie was not the type to get buried and neither was I.

* * *

That first week after the news was the hardest. The reality of Evie's hearing weighed on me heavily. I wondered if she might be instantly healed one day. I had heard of miracles like that happening. But now the question was how much could she hear and would it stay the same, or would she lose more hearing over time? Everything I read and researched showed that nothing was guaranteed until she got older and her test results were more consistent. The unknown was thick all around me, and I had to push it away or be suffocated by it.

I was never a closed person, and the energy I received from other people was often what kept me afloat each day. After the news, I told everyone, even before anyone had any questions. I told our story because I wanted to hear the words out loud. I needed it to be real, and I didn't want it to become any bigger in my head than what it really was.

Sensing that I was working through a lot in my heart, my mom gave me her complete CD set of Sheri Dew talks.[24] Listening to her helped me temporarily borrow some of her hope. I began to let go of the part of my will that believed Evie would be miraculously healed. I was starting to accept that she had hearing loss, but I still harbored some anger toward God for putting me through this. I felt disappointment, guilt, and mostly fear that I would not measure up as a mother. Emotionally, I was a mess, and I needed some extra help. Within a few days, I asked John for a priesthood blessing.

---

24 See *Sheri Dew Collection*, CD/DVD combo (Salt Lake City: Deseret Book, Sept. 2009).

In the blessing I was promised that my heart would change and be strengthened. I was blessed that I would feel the Lord's comfort and healing in His time. I was also reminded that through small and simple means are great things brought to pass. During this whole process, I felt like the Lord never left my side but was waiting for me to do something. I knew this trial could bury me if I let it, so I chose to do the small and simple things. I read scriptures and prayed and trudged forward with the little faith I could muster. I started to pray daily for my heart to change. I needed to accept this hearing loss as part of my daughter. How could she love and accept herself someday if I couldn't accept this part of her now? Each time I thought I had accepted it, I found myself praying for her hair to grow fast to hide the hearing aids she had to wear. Ashamed of myself, I would have to start praying for help to change my heart all over again.

The next few weeks were rough as Evie was tested in all sorts of ways to see if we could determine the cause of her hearing loss. Her doctors conducted genetic testing for a specific virus known to cause hearing defects. She also received an MRI to make sure there was not something missing from her inner ear, and we tested her eyes to make sure she could see well. It was not easy, but she was a wonderful baby and endured everything perfectly.

Every result came back negative. Evie was a healthy baby girl with a healthy body, and her permanent hearing loss was probably due to some gene we had yet to discover.

After all the tests, I savored the moments Evie was curled in my arms. I used to whisper and sing to her in her ears over and over, confident that what the audiologists had said was true: if I was close to Evie, she could hear my voice.

In the end, I believe Evie herself was the one who helped me accept everything. She grew up day by day with a strong, warm light in her eyes that brought me comfort. I grew used to our circumstances and our path. Evie blossomed around people and smiled more than most babies. When she looked at me, it felt backward, as if she knew I was worried and she wanted to tell me everything was going to be fine.

* * *

A few weeks after we learned about Evie's ears, my cousin sent me a little piece entitled "Welcome to Holland," written by Emily Pearl Kingsley: "I am often asked to describe the experience of raising a child with a disability—to try to help people who have not shared that unique experience to understand it, to imagine how it would feel. It's like this."[25] She then describes it like planning a trip to Italy. You get the guide book, you plan, you learn the language, and then you get off the plane and someone announces, "Welcome to Holland!"

Everything is different from what you planned for. The sights, the language, and the people are all different from what you were expecting. Not bad, just different.

We met a whole new group of people and learned a whole new language, including some American Sign Language. We learned more than we ever believed possible. And the Lord designed it that way. Slowly, by small steps, I was growing along with my daughter.

The next step after diagnosis was to get hearing aids. Evie had partial hearing, and everyone agreed it would be best to make the most of the hearing she already had. Through a tender mercy, John had a coworker who had recently been down the same road of hearing loss with her little son, who had Down syndrome, and she suggested we take advantage of the Utah School for the Deaf and Blind (USDB). The school had a loaner program, where babies and children could borrow a pair of hearing aids for a few months before parents decided where and how to purchase their own. New hearing aids were roughly $2,500 per ear and would last about five years. Health insurance did not help cover the cost.

The audiologist at Primary Children's Medical Center told us about another program through the state of Utah called the Early Fit program. To qualify for it, we had to apply for Medicaid and be denied, proving we were in a certain financial bracket. Then we would be eligible for a free pair of hearing aids. We weren't sure if it would work out, but we had to try. While we applied and waited for ridiculous amounts of paperwork to be processed, we went to the USDB to meet Christine, our new audiologist. In mid-April, she fitted Evie for a pair of loaner hearing aids.

Christine prepared us for Evie's reaction as she would finally be leaving the muffled state she was in to hear clearly with the new hearing aids. When Christine turned them on, Evie's eyes grew wide, and she got very quiet, listening to everything around her. It was a humbling sight, watching our little girl discover the sounds of her world. That night we went out to dinner to celebrate. Another couple waiting to be seated noticed Evie's ears and asked me how we found out our three-month-old daughter had hearing loss. I thought right then, *Thus it begins.*

---

25 Emily Pearl Kingsley, 1987, http://www.our-kids.org/archives/Holland.html.

At first I hated the whistling and squealing sounds the hearing aids made each time I got near my daughter to hug her or kiss her cheek. It was hard to learn how to put them in her ears, but we caught on after a week or so. Our biggest problem was simply getting her to keep the hearing aids in. Teething was a nightmare. The referred pain in her ears made it uncomfortable to wear the aids, and she would whip them out faster than we could sneeze. However, we knew the hearing aids were vital to Evie's speech and development, and she needed to have them in as much as possible. She wore an assortment of hats that tied under her chin to keep her hands away from the hearing aids. We also struggled to keep her ear molds fitting properly. Each time she grew, the ear molds would become loose, the hearing aids would squeal from the feedback, and we would have her fitted again for new molds. By the time those arrived in the mail, she would have a week before the whole process started again. I was a nanny that summer, and the girls I took care of were my greatest helpers. They watched over Evie and alerted me the moment she pulled out one of her "ears." My best days were when she would leave them in all day and I felt confident she had had full hearing that day.

In mid-September, we were approved for hearing aids through the Early Fit program, and Evie received her very own set. Another tender mercy from the Lord.

* * *

I decided after Evie was born that I would quit my job as a kindergarten teacher and stay home. It was not an easy decision for me, financially or emotionally. Yet I knew my priority, especially with everything that had happened, was to focus all my attention on Evie's development. My patriarchal blessing stressed that motherhood would be my most important accomplishment in this life. It felt hard to give up a career outside the home, but knowing what Evie needed from me reinforced that staying home was the right decision. I still had hopes to return to school to pursue higher education, but right then it wasn't about *my* education.

Soon after Evie was diagnosed with hearing loss, we got involved with the Parent Infant Program (PIP) through the USDB and a company called DDI Vantage. Both sent people into our home every two weeks to monitor Evie's verbal and physical progress. I learned about the varying degrees of hearing loss, starting with mild and going to moderate, severe, and then profound. I also learned about all the different devices available to those with any level of loss. Often children with hearing loss can have issues with balance, and DDI Vantage taught me how to encourage Evie's progress so she would have little to no problems with balance. I was seeing huge parts of a world I never knew existed.

Along with all this information, we were given a rather difficult choice. When a child was born with hearing loss, a parent had two roads to choose from. Either the child began American Sign Language (ASL) and embraced this new way of communication, or the child practiced what was called Listening and Spoken Language (LSL). With LSL, the child and parents embraced the technology available, such as hearing aids or cochlear implants. With the help of a speech therapist, they also worked on strengthening the neural pathways in the brain that control speech and language. We were being asked to choose our daughter's first language— English or American Sign Language.

The USDB sent us representatives from both to help us choose a path for Evie. One woman had been deaf most of her life, but after a cochlear implant, she was able to learn to speak. Another woman had been born deaf and had embraced ASL and Deaf culture.

John and I both loved the idea of ASL, and we wanted Evie to have this tool to speak to us whenever she needed to communicate. Along with ASL, there was a strong Deaf culture who believed their deafness helped define them. They were proud of and grateful for their path in life. I wanted that for Evie. I wanted her to be proud of who she was. However, in the end we didn't think it was right for our situation.

Evie was surrounded by a huge support system of *hearing* parents, friends, and family members. If we chose ASL, the entire support system would have to learn ASL to communicate with her. Evie's hearing loss was in the moderate range, which was right in the middle. She was not severely or profoundly deaf, and we didn't want to ignore the hearing she *did* have. We also believed the hearing loss was a part of her but not all of her. We were confident that if she would use the hearing aids and practice with a speech therapist, she would be able to secure the connections in her brain that would help her to communicate.

However, we did see the value in teaching her some baby sign language, and she learned to speak and sign to us at the same time. We were also grateful for the knowledge that if our situation changed, ASL was always available.

After choosing LSL, we were taught about the six "Ling" sounds and how to teach Evie to listen for them and identify them. Even as a baby, she caught on quickly. I was grateful I was a verbal, social person. I talked to Evie all the time, and now it was paying off. Not only was her language coming along beautifully, but physically, her development was perfect. Evie began walking (and running) at thirteen months. Our lives were full of visitors, doctor's appointments, and tests, but I got Evie out as much as possible to see friends and family. She was constantly surrounded by people and language.

* * *

Evie is three years old now, and her language and speech are exceptional. She knows some sign language, and her vocabulary grows by the minute. My daughter has also become the poster child for hearing aids. No matter where I am, I *always* get questions about why she wears such little hearing aids. When children ask what is on my daughter's ears, I simply say her ears work differently than ours do, and these little hearing aids help her hear everything we can.

The other day while I was at the park, I overheard a little girl telling her mom about the little girl over there that had things on her ears just like Grandpa. Children readily accept Evie, while adults give me a concerned look and ask more questions. After the questions, they see Evie's smile and the way she chatters at everyone, and it reaffirms to me and them that the largest of trials cannot extinguish the light in her.

One of my fears in the beginning was that she and I would never be able to enjoy music together. But Evie loves music. She sings with me. She sits at the piano and plays the keys with her little-girl fingers, making up songs just the way I did when I was her age. My daughter is a beautiful listener.

* * *

We are still no closer to finding out what caused her hearing loss. We will be meeting with genetic doctors in the future to rule out some other possibilities, but I don't mind not knowing anymore.

Recently, we had a doctor's appointment with Evie's ear, nose, and throat doctor. He asked questions and looked at her testing over the years. For a little while, we thought her hearing was better than we'd originally thought, but her last few tests have shown her hearing is at the same level it was when she was born.

When my husband asked the doctor what else we should do, the doctor simply stated, "You've done it. There isn't anything else now but to wait and see what happens." This would have been hard to hear at the beginning, but now it felt liberating. I told my husband I was comforted to know we had done everything. I could let go and turn this over to the Lord.

In the past, I struggled with worrying over the things I couldn't control. I used to misinterpret D&C 38:30: "If ye are prepared, ye shall not fear." I thought wrongly that if I worried about every scenario that *might* happen, I could somehow be ready for life's sucker punches and could tense before impact. I equated worry with being prepared. Even now I am tempted to worry that the bright light in Evie will get snuffed out one day by a bully at school and she will no longer be proud to be herself. But the Lord taught me a vital life lesson one day through another mother at the USDB who had several deaf children suffering with a genetic progressive hearing loss. She told me not to dwell on school and all my worries for the future. She told me to enjoy each moment I have with my daughter now. Since then, the Lord has taught me over and over the importance of choosing to surrender each day what I can't control. I choose the Lord each day. I choose happiness and peace instead of fear and despair. Over time, I have learned to trust His path for me, for my daughter, and for our family. I have had powerful witnesses that this is right for us and that this trial came to us for a reason.

Even the events leading up to Evie's birth bear witnesses of this. I was one week overdue when Evie was born, and because I was forty-one weeks pregnant, my doctor ordered a test to make sure the baby was healthy and safe while I waited to go into labor naturally. The test was conducted, and Evie's heart rate was not high enough. After I had a sugary drink, the nurse used a buzzer to create a loud sound on my belly, which should have made Evie jump. Due to her hearing loss, though, she didn't move. I was induced immediately. When Evie was delivered, it became clear that her umbilical cord was tied in a knot, and another few days of waiting for labor could have caused the knot to cinch the cord closed and create serious complications. We believe her hearing loss helped save her life.

* * *

Each night my daughter signs, "I love you." She smiles, and without a sound I sign back, "I love you!" I know my daughter has not lost a thing. She is perfect as she is. And I can love her perfectly.

Her middle name is Grace, and we believe that through God's grace, she came to us. Jesus Christ never left me alone, nor has He judged me for my weaknesses. Instead, He has unfolded tender mercies and blessings to me each day. I have never heard the Lord's voice with my natural ears, but that doesn't mean I can't hear Him or know He loves my daughter and me perfectly.

10
It's AA, Not ADD: My Son's Journey with Autism and Anxiety

by Liz Schultz

IN 1993, MY HUSBAND AND I married, and we planned, as most couples do, to have children in the next couple of years. My husband worked full time while attending premed classes at the University of Utah. I worked too, and together, with our minimum-wage jobs, we began to plan for the future.

Within a few short months, we discovered I was pregnant. With much joy, excitement, and anxiety about how we were going to manage a new baby, we announced the pregnancy to our parents. Fewer than forty-eight hours later, we were at a local hospital, where I hemorrhaged and lost the baby. We were heartbroken. At our follow-up appointment after the miscarriage, the doctor asked how long we wanted to wait before trying again and then wrote a prescription for birth control.

* * *

About a year later, we began the process of trying for a baby. We spent the next several years going to doctor's appointments, trying infertility medication, and ultimately learning that our chances of getting pregnant were about 0.05 percent on our own and only about 20 percent with expensive medical assistance. Again, we were heartbroken.

During this time, we constantly turned to the Lord in prayer, sometimes in faith and sometimes in great sorrow. I knew our desire to have a family was righteous, but it seemed that no matter what we tried, the answer was no.

We met with our bishop and received a referral to LDS Family Services. The process of getting ready for adoption was exciting but sometimes difficult. At the same time we turned our adoption paperwork in, our ward was divided, and I was called to be the Primary president. I was surprised at the calling since we were struggling to have children of our own. I worried that the Lord had put me in a position where I would continually be reminded of what was missing in my life. But I was wrong. I didn't want a three-year-old; I wanted a baby. Being around those sweet spirits in Primary was a healing blessing to me. I found that I especially loved the children who seemed to struggle with Primary. I loved trying to reach out and connect with them.

I found that interesting because one concern we faced with adoption was not knowing if the child would have special concerns. Would we be up to that kind of challenge? Eric and I had both independently felt that we would have a child with special needs, but it wasn't until after we had been blessed with children that we talked about those feelings.

I really struggled with infertility and then the process of accepting that our children would have to come in a different way. I found myself turning inward rather than turning to Eric. I didn't want to burden him with my constant longing for a family; I didn't feel he truly understood my heartache and didn't want him to feel like he was not doing enough to make that happen. I kept trying to pull closer to my Heavenly Father, but I knew I was emotionally pulling away from Eric, and I didn't like it. I didn't know how to reach out to him for love and support, so I didn't. I kept myself busy getting paperwork ready and prayed constantly for a birth mother to choose us.

In 2000, we were blessed with a son, and he was perfect. Words cannot describe the joy we felt as we held our little Todd in our arms and realized the dream of becoming parents. About fifteen months later, we were blessed with a little girl, Heather, Todd's full biological sister. It was such an amazing experience. Our medical knowledge of the birth parents gave only the fact that the birth mother had been diagnosed as being bipolar. We had no written history, and so began our parenting experience with no preconceived expectations, a take-it-as-it-comes-and-love-it approach.

* * *

By the time Todd was three years old, we were having him tested for speech delay, which resulted in his qualifying for preschool services. By the end of first grade, he was experiencing separation anxiety at school. In second grade, he could get really silly, standing on his desk and singing songs in the middle of class and other times walking around the classroom, taking kids' papers off their desks, wadding them up, and throwing them across the room. We also started to see changes in him at home and church, mostly with mood swings. There was one day at church when Todd ran out of his Primary class with three teachers chasing after him to make sure he was going to be okay. I was able to get him back in the building, and then I found an empty classroom where I could turn off the lights and let the dark quiet surround him as he tried to calm down.

I was grateful for teachers who rallied around my son to make sure he was okay, but as they asked what to do and what would help, I was at a loss. I didn't know what to do when he got upset. It was like watching someone have a seizure. I had to wait for the mood swing to pass, and I kept him safe and tried to remove the audience. I asked that they come get me when he was upset so I could come and help him, and I continually reached out for the Spirit to guide me with each mood swing. What tone should I use? What should I talk about? Were the lights too bright? Was it too hot or cold? I would wait to be guided through every aspect of the meltdown.

I loved this little boy with all my heart and needed Heavenly Father's help to know what to do. I was never left without direction. I always seemed to know what to do. It was hard to explain it to others who worked with Todd, to say the Spirit let me know what to do and that I had to trust the promptings. Not everyone was able to do that, and I worried people would think I was a little too churchy.

* * *

It was at this point that we started to seek medical help. Even with the addition of medication and a psychiatrist, Todd still had problems in school. I was on a first-name basis with the principal, and one day, as an example, the principal called to tell me, "Todd is running laps in the halls and won't stop."

Todd already had an individualized education program (IEP) set up for bipolar disorder, which created additional accommodations in the school. The principal, teachers, and I had created it. We had determined what things Todd struggled with at school, what needed extra attention, and what we could do to help in those areas. Those accommodations allowed him to go to the special needs room when he could not function in class.

As we ended the school year, Todd was starting to feel that he was the bad kid and was always in trouble. His behavior was fine at home but not at school, and we were trying to determine the difference between the two environments. I continually prayed to know how to help Todd understand the differences between him and the other kids, that walking by someone and kicking them in the leg just because they were sitting there was not a good choice and that other choices were better. I prayed to know how to help him see that he was still a good kid even though things were hard for him. I still constantly relied on the Spirit to direct each of my words.

I found that I was using this communication with the Spirit to get to know my son, to let Heavenly Father teach me what Todd needed to hear and who he was on the inside. The teachers and administrators would ask what they could do to better help Todd. Again, my answer was always that I didn't know.

Obviously, I couldn't ask them to simply follow the Spirit every day in class with him or tell them Heavenly Father would direct them to know what to say and do. I let them know Todd needed to feel accepted by them no matter what he did and if he felt that, he would be more likely to trust them. I prayed for the teachers and the principal to be directed to know what to do. I knew they had been to school and had received a lot of training, and I prayed that thoughts would come about things they had learned or seen that could help Todd, and I paid attention as they tried something new at school in case I needed to use it at home.

* * *

A couple years earlier, a charter school had been built about a block from our home. It was called Spectrum Academy. Its charter was for children with high-functioning autism. Although Todd's diagnosis was bipolar disorder with ADHD, I picked up an application for Spectrum but still worried that if he attended there he might pick up other inappropriate behaviors. Then we would have to try to address the behaviors we were already dealing with and a whole bunch of new ones. We prayed that Heavenly Father would help us know what to do.

A week before Todd started third grade, I got a call that he was accepted into the charter school. Eric and I took some time to visit the school and find out more about it. I talked to them about Todd not having autism but having bipolar disorder, and they reassured me that the diagnosis was one they were familiar with and comfortable working with. They explained that most of the students at the school had multiple diagnoses and that they could handle it.

We prayed to know if we should accept the spot and felt a strong confirmation that this was the plan for Todd. We started sending him to this school and Heather to the other school. Heather would walk with her friends, and I would walk with Todd to make sure he got to class okay. Within just a few weeks, Todd was settling in and coming home happy. He would say, "I'm not the worst kid—somebody else got in trouble today."

I think it was at this point that Heather started feeling the difference of having a sibling with special needs. Kids at school would ask her why her brother didn't go to school with her. It was hard for her to know how to answer that question. How could she say she had a brother who sometimes struggled and not have them think something was wrong with him? How could she explain at seven years old what bipolar disorder was and that Todd was a great brother? It was hard for us as parents to know what to do to help her and what to have her say.

At the same time, our stake was split, and a new stake was created. I was called to be the stake Primary president. I was sure that trying to select counselors and a secretary was going to be challenging. Although I knew many people, there were so many more I didn't know, and I wanted to make sure I called the individuals the Lord needed to serve with me.

I was surprised that it took less than an hour to think of the names of my counselors and secretary. I didn't know anything about my second counselor or secretary, and the only thing I knew about my first counselor was that I had once heard she worked at my son's school. I was excited about the experiences I could bring to my calling and was humbled by the fact that there were so many children I would have an opportunity to serve. I knew the Lord had prepared me for the calling, but I had no idea why it was happening at this point in my life.

* * *

About two months into fourth grade, Todd started having problems again. He started having huge separation anxiety every morning at the start of school. There were some days that it could take up to an hour for me to get him to transition. By the end of winter, we started seeing aggression issues. He would get frustrated and overwhelmed and start yelling, throwing books, knocking desks over, and running from the classroom. Within a few short weeks, Todd was becoming a danger to himself and others at school. There were several times I was called to the school because Todd was experiencing such intense meltdowns that we had to physically restrain him to keep him safe. One time he kicked the teacher and could not calm down. My husband was at the school with him that day, and they gave him the option to contact the police to see if that would help Todd recognize the severity of all that was happening. They also called me and asked me to come to the school while we waited for the police to arrive.

I cannot express how hard it was not to gather Todd in my arms but to stand back and wait for the police to come. The officer was remarkable and understood the student base of Spectrum Academy. He talked to Todd and explained that the police were his friends, but if he couldn't stay in control of his actions, the police would have to come help. Todd was able to calm down enough that he could come home with us.

About a week later, it was determined that Todd was not safe in school and could not return until he received additional treatment. Because we all knew Todd could not function in a traditional school, the principal assured us that when Todd was ready to come back, he would have a spot even if they had to bring another desk in for him. In looking for ways we could help Todd without the structure of a school system, we contacted our insurance company and were told about Primary Children's Residential Treatment Center. We were given the needed authorization, contacted the RTC, and were placed on a waiting list.

I worked from home, which was the only reason I continued to work while having young children. Most of my work hours were while my kids were in school, and I was there for them every afternoon when they got home. I didn't want to give up such an incredible work situation, and I loved what I did and the positive impact it had on those I worked with, but I was ready to quit and do whatever it took to take care of Todd. I prayed all the time to know if the Lord wanted me to make that move or stay employed so I could influence those I worked with and provide added income for our family.

As I thought about my work options, I decided I would find out everything they did in a residential treatment center and just do it at home because there was no way I could send my son away. But then I thought about Todd and Heather's birth mom and the courage it had taken for her to place them where it would be best for them. I remembered the time of placement and the tears and aching she felt as she placed those precious children in our arms. After realizing the sacrifices she had made for them, I told Heavenly Father I was willing to do what was best for Todd, even if it meant he would not be with me. And then I sobbed, knowing that choosing that path would be extremely difficult. I prayed for and felt the peace and comfort that only the Spirit can give. Eric and I both knew the Lord wanted us to follow this path.

* * *

Eric and I were feeling the pressure of having a child with special needs in our marriage. Each of us was trying to follow the feelings and promptings we were receiving, and we didn't always agree on what to do in each situation. I tended to try to simply understand what Todd was feeling and connect in a way that would help him process what was happening. Eric tended to address each behavior as it came and stop it, letting Todd know it was not appropriate. Todd needed both, but it was sometimes hard to have Eric handle a situation differently than I would want to on my own.

At these times I looked back on the adoption process and how I had stopped reaching out to Eric. I didn't ever want that separation to happen again. I knew we could either grow closer with trials or let them push us apart, and I made a decision that I would not let them drive us apart. I prayed for help in accepting that we did things differently and that Heavenly Father would inspire each of us differently. I also consciously accepted that Eric had been chosen to be Todd's father just as much as I'd been chosen to be his mother. I needed to respect Eric's role as a father and support him.

Thankfully, Eric was a righteous priesthood holder who was also looking to Heavenly Father for guidance and inspiration. We both understood that this precious son was actually Heavenly Father's and that Heavenly Father loved him very much. We each had to put aside our pride in thinking that we could come up with the perfect solution and reach toward each other for support and to our Heavenly Father for direction. We had to be willing to let the other person lead sometimes and try both of our ideas. Our personalities worked well together. Each of us tried to make the best of every situation. We understood there were times we weren't going to agree, but we kept working through the problems. It was with this team effort that we realized our situation with Todd was bigger than both of us and that we could not do it on our own.

* * *

One day my sisters wanted to take my kids to the zoo to give me a break. I knew that could be a challenge for Todd, so I sat down with my sisters before they left and showed them how to restrain him safely if he became violent. I instructed them to call me so I could come get him if there were problems.

I began to recognize how bad things were—how that was not something typical parents had to deal with. Many of my neighbors were incredibly supportive during this time. Some of them had siblings or children with special needs, so they were sensitive to Todd's feelings and were supportive of our family. Others struggled with our situation.

There was one dear friend who didn't have that background and didn't understand Todd. She had children around my children's ages and was concerned that if Todd had a meltdown, he would hurt her children. She said her children were not allowed to play at our home when Todd was home, which was devastating. I loved my little boy; he wasn't some kind of monster who tried to hurt others. He just got overwhelmed and needed more love. I felt like she doubted my ability to be attuned to my son and where he was emotionally so I could keep her children safe. I was angry that she was not being more Christlike and reaching out to him and me in love.

* * *

We continued getting updates from Todd's psychiatrist.

Unfortunately, she didn't think I was being completely up front and honest with her about everything that was happening, that maybe I was exaggerating, and therefore she didn't think it was as severe as it was.

Todd wanted to go back to school and would try to sneak out of the house to walk down there. It was tricky to find times to shower because I was afraid he would take off. Additionally, Todd had to be physically restrained at least once a day to keep everyone safe. Because the psychiatrist didn't understand what was going on and our wait to get into a treatment program seemed never ending, I began videotaping Todd's meltdowns.

It is hard to explain what it felt like to ask neighbors to help, but I would carry a little video camera with me everywhere and ask a neighbor or someone else to record meltdowns while I restrained my son so he wouldn't hurt me or himself.

One day, just before an appointment with the psychiatrist, I knew Todd was going to have problems because he didn't want to go. When his meltdown started, I pulled out the camera and started recording Todd running to the neighbor's house, yelling, and trying to hit me. Then he fell to the ground, still yelling that he was not going to go. At that point, I sent Heather to get a neighbor to help me put Todd in the car. I then had Heather tape the event as the neighbor and I carried Todd to the car, put him in, and turned on the safety locks so we could leave.

I remember driving to the appointment in tears, thinking, *She's going to have to admit one of us.* When we got to the psychiatrist's office, I explained what had happened, and she seemed a little concerned. Then I showed her the video, and her eyes got big.

"Oh, I think he needs residential treatment," she said.

She then tried to get a hold of the on-call doctor but with no luck. She prescribed some additional medication to help Todd calm down, and then we waited for a phone call from the RTC with an opening. The medication did not help much, and Todd continued to spiral downward. Our only option at that point was to wait for a call or have him admitted through the emergency room. We decided we would go home and wait to see if she could contact the on-call doctor to try to speed up the process.

* * *

We were at our wits' end just trying to get through each day. I prayed for strength that I could continue to face each challenge. I prayed that Todd would have times of peace and that I could be a strength to him. I prayed that Heather would somehow understand what was going on and that her needs would be met.

I knew she wasn't getting the attention she needed, and I didn't know how to change that. I had to keep facing each challenge as it came up, and I had to focus on Todd's needs. One night, our family went out for dinner, and while we were eating, Todd got really mad at Heather. He held his knife and fork in his hands and said, "I just want to kill her." We took away the silverware, and I sat between the kids.

We continued to eat, but I knew it was difficult for nine-year-old Heather to understand what was going on. I was grateful that through ordeals like this and so many other issues, she was still welcome to play with her friends at our neighbors' homes. She loved them, and it was great that she could find peace for herself playing with them.

* * *

As I continued to serve in my stake calling, I began to recognize the amazing blessing I had been given to serve the children. The Lord knew I would need a lot of extra help during this time and was able to bless me because of my service. Although I loved all the work I was doing with the children, my favorite part of my calling was participating in stake council meetings. It was an incredible blessing to be surrounded by brothers and sisters of such faith and fortitude.

We would start each meeting studying from the scriptures. I reveled in the Spirit as we spoke of different doctrines, and I acutely felt the testimonies around me. My spiritual cup was filled to overflowing as I also testified of the gospel and my experiences with it.

At the end of each meeting, we would identify specific names to pray for. People mentioned names but not always reasons—sometimes it was for challenges they were facing, and other times it was in gratitude for answered prayers. Each time, someone asked that we pray for my family.

I would often tear up as whoever was praying would say my family's name out loud. I could feel the strength of those prayers and the faith in our behalf. I felt honored to be among such noble brothers and sisters who continued to reach out and pray for me.

Those were not the only prayers sent our way. My dear friend's mother regularly put our names on the temple prayer roll, and my own mother added our names to the prayer roll too. Our names were never off that list.

It was interesting because Mondays always seemed to be a little bit of a challenge, and then Tuesdays would be easier. I realized it was because the temples where our names were on the rolls were closed on Mondays.

There were times a sweet family in our ward would stop by to give us homemade caramel popcorn. They knew how much Todd loved that, and it touched my heart that they would take the time to minister to our sweet son and give so much to our family.

* * *

On June 16, 2010, after six weeks of living in crisis on the waiting list, Todd was admitted to Primary Children's Residential Treatment Center.

For me it was a little like sending Todd off to his own special MTC . . . at ten years old. For weeks, Todd had begged to go to the hospital because he knew he needed help. He had cried and asked me to call the hospital, telling me to tell them we would pay extra money if he could go now. And the day had come.

This is an excerpt from my journal that day:

> Today was one of the hardest days Eric and I have ever faced. I got up and made breakfast, and Todd was up not much after me, asking how soon we would be leaving. I let him know, and he turned on the Wii for some last-minute playtime.
>
> We said family prayer this morning just before we left, extending the safety of our home to each person, no matter where they were, and then loaded up in the van. When we got to April's house to drop Heather off, the girls gave Todd hugs and gave him a picture to take with him of his two little cousins. Todd and Heather gave each other one last hug, and Heather kissed Todd on the check as they said their good-byes.
>
> We listened to music as we made the drive up to Research Park by the U, and Todd played air guitar to the Eagles' "Hotel California." His uncle called to let him know he would be thinking about him and that he loved him.
>
> As we pulled into the parking lot at Primary's residential treatment building, Eric asked what we should name the destination in the GPS, and Todd yelled out, "Todd's Home." We decided we would list it as "Primary's" instead, and all went in to start the admit process.
>
> The friendliest nurse greeted us within minutes, and then we met the LCSW (licensed clinical social worker), Craig, who will be in charge of Todd while he is there. Todd played with toys for a few minutes, laid on the couch, and was really bored as we worked our way through all the paperwork that needed to be done. He said he was hungry, so Craig (the LCSW) took him down to the kitchen area, where the kids were still having breakfast. Craig came back, and we continued with paperwork, and then the nurse and the nurse practitioner came in to meet with us.

Craig left for a few minutes, coming back to report that Todd was already heading into meltdown and that he'd tried to bolt from the area to get back to Mom and Dad. He was reassured that Mom and Dad would be down in a few minutes.

We talked to the nurse and the nurse practitioner about what to expect with what they would be doing and then talked to the nurse practitioner about Todd's meds and what our goals are with treatment. We then went for a tour of the building, finding Todd up against a door, yelling that he wanted out.

They tried to work with him on activities and other things, but he was not about to work with them. I picked him up (all one hundred pounds) and told him he could go on the tour with us. We got a little ways before transferring him to Eric's back for a piggyback ride. That did not last long before he was so angry he was trying to choke Eric and bite his back. So back on the floor we went, with me holding him facing away from me to try to help him get calmed back down. He was so mad.

He said he hated this place and that everyone was mean to him. He wanted to go to the regular hospital, where he could stay in bed all day and have them bring him his food there. I explained to him that he would have lots of time in his room but that they would be eating all together in the kitchen area.

Well, he was not appeased, and since he wasn't calming down but was continuing to try to break free and become a safety threat, he was able to spend some time in the time-out room. It is a small room where the kids cannot break anything and where the staff can lock the door and monitor the child through the window higher in the door. We have never heard Todd kick and hit anything so hard. He was yelling and hitting, so we determined that we would continue the tour without him, giving him a chance to calm down a little before we needed to say good-bye.

As we left Todd in the isolation room and headed upstairs to see his room, Craig asked us if what had just happened was what we had been calling meltdowns for the last six weeks. We said yes, and Craig said, "Oh, I'm sorry." We could tell he really meant it, and that, apparently, what we considered a meltdown was much worse than what some other parents were calling meltdowns.

"Todd will have his own room with a built-in desk and shelves for him to put things on. He will like it in a few days when he gets adjusted. They have a big gym area, a common area attached to the kitchen area, and even a place where the kids can go play video games and an arcade machine. There is a big playground outside that he'll be able to use once he can safely go outside. There are a lot of great activities for them and a great staff to help them."

After our tour, we picked up our stuff from the room we were meeting in and headed back up to see if Todd had calmed enough that we could say good-bye. He was still crying but was safe enough that we could go in with him. He just cried and said he didn't want to stay and asked us not to leave him. I explained to him, as I have for the last several weeks, that there are going to be hard times, especially the next few days, but that he would be okay. I let him know we would call him tonight and that we will come visit him on Saturday. He clung to me, sobbing for me not to leave him. Before handing him off to Eric, we had a family hug, and then I then left the room to try to keep myself as pulled together as possible while Eric said his good-byes.

Craig was there so Eric could leave, and as we left the room, Todd clung to Craig. So handing Todd off to the team became very literal for him. We left the building and just cried. We cried as we drove, and we held each other's hands. This is not a fun part of parenting.

So that is the rundown of this morning. Not fun at all. We know this is where Todd needs to be right now and that the people at the treatment center will be best able to work with him and help him gain some better coping skills and find some med combinations that will best help him.

As we drove away, we literally left him with total strangers. We had to trust that they would take care of our son for us when we could not. We had to have faith that Heavenly Father would help everything be okay. We were so heartbroken to have to leave our little boy and yet overwhelmed with feelings of gratitude that we had finally been able to get him into the program where he could start to receive the help he so desperately needed.

We continued on each day, trying to follow the lead of the RTC staff. We began to better understand their processes and how we could be as supportive as possible to help Todd know we loved him and were proud of him for all the things he was trying to learn.

We also found another great support at this time. A couple of years earlier, we'd lost our yellow lab, Brittany, who had come into our family during our experience with infertility. She was our "first child," and her loss had been hard on the family, but with Todd away from us, we talked about how Brittany could now be with him at the RTC. We prayed that Heavenly Father would allow her to be with Todd, and there were many times we felt her spirit there. More importantly, Todd felt her there and found great comfort in knowing he was not alone.

* * *

We had to do our best to call Todd before 8:00 p.m., as several of the medications he was on made him sleepy. On the nights we called and he was asleep, we asked the staff to leave a message that we had called. We didn't ever want him starting the day thinking we had forgotten about him.

We never forgot him. During the time Todd was gone, we lived in survival mode. Honestly, I don't remember many details of the months he was not with us. Even now I don't think I am really ready to remember all of it. I wrote only a few entries in my journal during that time, and these are a few of the thoughts I put down:

> June 29, 2010
> The phone calls every day and the visits twice a week are really helping us a lot. It is good to talk to him about how his day went and what things are happening here.
>
> He still has days where he has time-outs, but he has not been in isolation for about a week now, and that is really good. They are doing summer school for about three hours a day. Some days are pretty good, but yesterday he

was feeling overwhelmed with math and had a hard time. He said he was in time-out twice and that he slept in the time-out room one of the times. Sad to think that my little boy is sleeping in a tiled room, but it is good that he was able to calm down again.

He is so looking forward to moving from high to moderate, or "mod," as he calls it. That will give him some more privileges, such as going outside and riding bikes. Then we will work toward low so we can have off-campus visits.

July 31, 2010

Today we finally got to take Todd off campus. It has been forty-five days since we dropped Todd off, and I was beginning to feel like he would never get to "low" so we could leave campus. We love the visits on campus—being able to go down to the gym, to the arcade room, and playing outside—but there was something to signing the paper that we were taking responsibility for him, that we could load him into the car, and that we could go somewhere as a family. It has been so hard driving away after each visit and knowing that we were leaving him behind. Today was the first time in nearly two months that we didn't have to leave him behind as we drove out of the parking lot. It was amazing.

We went and watched *Toy Story 3*. We were so excited to go because we often went to movies before he went into the RTC. We were so excited to pick up our popcorn and drinks and head into the theatre. Little did I know that the movie we were about to watch was going to be one of the hardest movies I would ever watch. I bawled through most of it, thinking about how Todd was growing up and changing and I wasn't even there for most of it. As we headed back to the RTC, the kids asked why I was sad, and I said I was just happy that we could all be together.

As Eric and I reflected on that first time we were able to take Todd off campus, we remembered that by the end of the movie, Todd was actually anxious to get back to the RTC. He needed the consistency and the more isolated feeling. It was comforting to him. He loved being able to spend the time with us but recognized that he was benefiting from his time at the center. We were grateful that he felt at home and safe there.

September 1, 2010

It is hard to believe Todd has been in residential treatment for eleven weeks today. We are seeing progress, but, as expected, it is very slow. Two steps forward and then one step back seems to be the pattern we are in. Sometimes he goes for a week or so without having to go to isolation, and then other times he is in there two to three times a week.

Even though the staff does their best to get Todd's glasses away from him when he is going into a meltdown, my optometrist knows me by sight now because we have to send a pair of glasses in every three weeks or so to be replaced. And these are the more expensive glasses that can take most anything. Someday someone will make indestructible glasses, and we will get them and give them a run for their money.

Most days I am good, keeping insanely busy and focusing on my faith that Heavenly Father is very aware of Todd and that Todd is right where he needs to be. Other days I just fall apart—like last night. I can feel it taking its toll on me as the process continues on and on.

We actually got to bring him home for a few hours on Sunday, and that was wonderful! But then we had to take him back, and I noticed a little bit more the emptiness of his not being here.

Heather is doing well and loves being back in school. We have enjoyed the one-on-one time with her. It has been amazing watching her grow in this experience. She has matured in many areas, and it has been wonderful. It is neat to watch her pray for Todd to come back home when he is ready and to see them interact on our visits. She is really growing up, and it is fun being a part of that.

* * *

On Wednesday, October 6, we got to bring Todd home. We were walking on air as we placed his belongings in the van, gave the staff hugs, and loaded up—as a whole family—to go home.

Although we continued to have Todd attend RTC Monday through Friday, 8:00 a.m. to 5:00 p.m., for the next three months, we were so excited to have everyone home at night, under the same roof. We threw a big party with all the neighbors to celebrate Todd's homecoming. It was fun to share something so exciting with all of them.

* * *

As Todd continued his day treatment, we were blessed with the opportunity to have neuropsych testing done. We discovered that Todd was actually not bipolar; he had high-functioning autism. He also had anxiety disorder and other diagnoses. Although it was nice to have a better understanding of the challenges he faced, our approach of reaching out to him in love and understanding while relying on the Spirit to direct us did not change. That was where we found peace in the challenges we faced.

Some of the things we took away from the experience of having Todd gone and of meeting with the social worker each week helped change how we approached things. First, we realized our family reacted differently than a lot of families did. Typically, those weekly meetings were great opportunities for family counseling. For us, they were an opportunity to hear what the week was like for Todd from the caregivers' point of view and to learn how we could apply helpful methods at home. We were willing to be teachable, and we relied on the Lord for direction and knew the answers came from many resources, not just our own limited knowledge.

We also came to understand that we were not trying to fix Todd. There was nothing wrong with him. He had challenges different from our own, but we had faith that Heavenly Father would teach us about those differences and help Todd find joy in life. We accepted that he was Heavenly Father's son, and we respected that there was a plan for him.

* * *

I have come to understand that this life and Heavenly Father's plan are really pretty simple. I chose His plan in the premortal life, and that allowed me to come to earth. He asks that I choose His plan again, which means that as a parent I need to help my children learn the plan so they can also choose it. If my children never master math, science, language, sports, etc., that doesn't mean I am a failure as a mother. All I have to worry about is creating opportunities for them to feel the Spirit and teaching them about our Heavenly Father and His infinite love for them.

I often teach them about the Atonement of Jesus Christ and the covenants they can make with God. I encourage and love them, but I know I also have to step back because it is not my role to save them. That is the Savior's role. I do all in my power to teach them and then allow the Savior to fill His role and make up the difference. As long as I hold on to that, I feel the peace and joy of knowing that I am about my Father's work. I am helping bring to pass the immortality and eternal life of those whose lives I can touch. I play my part but recognize that it is His work and that I am just a helper.

I have come to understand that all the things I learned growing up about children don't always apply. My children are individuals, and the techniques I use to help teach them are just as individual. I am grateful for inspiration to know how to implement the right practices and for the opportunity I have each day to learn from my Heavenly Father about the amazing children I have been blessed with.

Elder Lynn G. Robbins gave one of my favorite conference talks. He talks about different parenting classes we might have here on earth:

> A sweet and obedient child will enroll a father or mother only in Parenting 101. If you are blessed with a child who tests your patience to the nth degree, you will be enrolled in Parenting 505. Rather than wonder what you might have done wrong in the premortal life to be so deserving, you might consider the more challenging child a blessing and opportunity to become more godlike yourself. With which child will your patience, long-suffering, and other Christlike virtues most likely be tested, developed, and refined? Could it be possible that you need this child as much as this child needs you?[26]

I have often thought of having a T-shirt made that says, "Currently enrolled in parenting 505."

I am grateful for the blessing of having a child with special needs. I am grateful to know I am not the only parent in the class and that there are many who understand what I go through each day. Even more than that, I am grateful for the support I receive constantly from Heavenly Father. He blesses me with friends and neighbors who love us and strengthen us, and even my dear friend who would not allow her kids

---

26 "What Manner of Men and Women Ought Ye to Be?" *Ensign*, May 2011.

to be around Todd now lets them play at my home. Choosing to not let negative experiences affect my ability to have positive interactions has helped me reach out in love to those who do not yet understand.

To this day we speak of the RTC with fondness, and though Todd has been home for a year and a half, he still wants to go up and visit the staff. It was one of the hardest things we've gone through, but it brought our family back together. We are again able to experience the joy of being together, of Todd not having meltdowns each day, and of all of us enjoying life again. We have all changed. The experience has taught us much about compassion, patience, and loving the individual. I appreciate more every day that my family is together, because I know what it is like to have someone gone. I appreciate that I am not alone as a mother, that there is a Heavenly Father who blesses us with people and experiences when we need them most.

* * *

Todd's meltdowns are infrequent now. Some of the change is that we understand what things are hard for Todd and how we can help him when he feels those challenges. A lot of it is Todd's desire and fortitude to keep trying, even when it is hard.

We continue to see a therapist and utilize medication to help with his levels. There are still times when I end up at school with him. Thankfully, the school was able to get my laptop on their system so I can still work as I sit next to him in class. There are Sundays when Todd can't handle church, and we address that as it comes. But even with that challenge, Todd has received the priesthood and has had opportunities to serve others, and I am so proud of him for that.

As I look to Todd's teenage years and beyond, I do it with the same approach I always have: I have no idea what will happen, but I'll take it a day and a prayer at a time. We hope Todd will be able to serve a mission in some fashion and that he will find a loving companion he can be sealed to in the temple. I know he looks forward to being a father and will love having children of his own. We don't know how or if any of that will happen, but we turn to Heavenly Father, knowing He has a special plan for each of His children—including Todd. And we are excited to find out what that plan is.

11

Death of My Husband: Finding My Happily Ever After Again

by Lorraine Robinson Mason

I DON'T THINK ANYTHING CAN ever fully prepare a person for the sting that hits when their spouse dies. Looking back on it, though, I can truly see how the Lord laid out for me many tender mercies of preparation.

About six months before my husband, Robbie, died, he and I had a random conversation about what I should do if he died at a young age, leaving me with four young children to raise. He laid out plans for me regarding our business and our finances, and he expressed that he wanted me to marry again when the time was right. It was important to him that I still have someone in my life to love and to help take care of our children and me. He wanted to make sure I knew I had his blessing to find a great man to love again. I was completely thrown off by the conversation but felt comforted and at peace knowing what his wishes were for us in his absence.

I never could have imagined how soon I would be living the very life we had just discussed. When I was thirty-two, my worst nightmare came true—my husband, also thirty-two, passed away suddenly in the night. Our children were eleven, seven, five, and three.

Despair, emptiness, and heartbreak became my constant companions. I didn't personally know anyone else who had gone through this, so I had no idea what to expect or what to do in this situation, but I did have a friend who had recently helped a cousin through a similar situation, and she was able to give me some advice on what I should do. I was so grateful to have that help and direction because I was in total shock and couldn't keep my thoughts clear and focused. All I could think about was how hard and lonely this new life of ours was going to be. I missed my sweet husband so much and felt sick and empty and sad.

I had to try to keep it together and be strong for my children, but sometimes it was so hard to do. One day, about a month after my husband's death, I was sitting in my kitchen when my seven-year-old daughter came home from school crying. She had gotten in trouble for "helping the teacher too much," which meant she was talking out of turn and trying to keep the other kids in the classroom on task. As she sat in tears explaining things to me, I looked into her sad little face through tears of my own and realized how much my little girl needed her daddy. He was the one who understood her the best, not me. He could fix everything that went wrong in her life. I was the one who butted heads with her over almost everything because our personalities were so similar. I saw in her what bothered me about myself. But Robbie loved her for who she was: a miniature me.

I didn't know how I was going to be the parent she needed me to be. I began to feel that I somehow had to be a good enough mother to make up for my children not having a father anymore. But I also knew this was a task I would fail at day after day. There was simply no way I alone could mend our broken hearts.

* * *

As time went on, friends and neighbors around me went on with their normal lives while I continued to feel like mine was over. I often felt lost and alone. At times I felt jealous when I saw my friends holding hands with their spouses or when our friends had couples outings and I was no longer invited because my other half was gone. I felt angry and bitter when I heard other women complain about their husbands leaving their dirty clothes on the bedroom floor or not helping enough with the children or the housework. I could only wish my husband was still here to leave his mess for me to step over or clean up. I longed for the toilet seat to be left up, the shoes to not be put where they belonged, and the covers on his side of the bed to be left unmade.

My bed was cold and lonely. Many nights I felt so sad and alone that I couldn't fall asleep, so I would go into the bedroom of one of my children, cradle their sleeping body in my arms, and quietly carry them into my bed. I needed to hear the gentle breathing and feel the warmth of a sweet little one sleeping next to me. Some mornings it was so hard to get out of bed knowing all the things I needed to do that day. I felt overwhelmed with day-to-day tasks. I needed to keep moving and do my best to keep our home in order to maintain some sort of stability for my children, but some days it felt totally impossible, and all I wanted to do was lie in my bed and cry—I just wanted to give up.

* * *

But gradually I came to realize how strong my testimony in the Savior Jesus Christ really was and what the purpose in having such a testimony was. Without Him and the gift of the Atonement, our new lives would be absolutely unbearable. I quickly came to understand what the phrase "angels among us" meant to me because I viewed all of my family and friends as those angels.

It truly is through other people that our Father in Heaven helps us, provides for our needs, and answers our prayers. I could not have survived day after day without so many wonderful people reaching out to us with kind words and selfless acts of service. I saw in so many people the type of person I wanted to be someday. I wanted to learn to serve others the way my family was being served. I wanted to be the kind of friend who deserved to have so many friends come to my rescue. I wanted to better learn how to lighten the burdens of those around me the way our burdens were being lightened.

* * *

As the realization of my need to provide for my children set in, so did a lot of anxiety about how I would make that happen. I was so grateful my husband had spent the thirteen years of our marriage building a good business that provided well for our family. I was also grateful that for the past seven years I had had the opportunity to work with him from home as I raised our little family. I knew many of the ins and outs of the business, so it wasn't totally foreign to me, especially the financial end of it, and we had many good people already in place and had established other aspects so things could run smoothly while I adjusted to everything that was happening.

I was so grateful to those who stepped in and helped make it all happen. I tried to take care of as much of the business needs as possible while my children were in school so I could focus on their needs without interruption when they got home. It was a tricky balancing act, but with a lot of help from friends and family, we made it work the best we could.

* * *

About eighteen months after my husband's passing, my children and I found out we had been betrayed by two people who were very close to us, who had promised us they would do everything they could to keep the business running and help my children and me in our time of need. I had trusted them with the business while I'd focused more on taking care of my children, but when I found out they had been spending much of their time conspiring to take my business for themselves and had been successful in doing so, my heart shattered; I was totally blindsided by their greed, selfishness, and dishonesty.

Not realizing it was possible, I felt even lower than I had when my husband died. I wanted to die myself. I felt like I couldn't live another day, like things were totally hopeless. One day I sat in my car in the garage, thinking about ways I could leave this earth life, but the thought of my four sweet little children being without a father and a mother stopped me. I couldn't put them through another death. My thoughts were incredibly dark and selfish. Deep down I knew that was not the Lord's plan for me.

At that moment, my brother called me. He said he was calling because I was on his mind. He told me he knew I was going through a really hard time and wanted me to know Heavenly Father was there for me to talk to and that through the Atonement, I could get through anything that came my way.

I immediately went up to my room and knelt in prayer. I poured out my heart to Father and asked Him to help me know what I needed to do in this incredibly ugly situation. He knew exactly what I was going through, and He was where I needed to turn for help. I felt that I needed to begin a fast for direction and healing.

Before then, I had always fasted on the appropriate Sunday but had never truly known what the commandment meant or the power behind it.

The day following my fast, the moment I got out of bed I felt a tangible weight had been lifted from my shoulders. It was as though I was floating. Nothing in my situation had changed, but my mind was clear and my sad, broken heart was beginning to mend. It made me think of the scripture Mosiah 24:14: "And I will also ease the burdens which are put upon your shoulders, that even you cannot feel them upon your backs, even while you are in bondage; and this will I do that ye may stand as witnesses for me hereafter, and that ye may know of a surety that I, the Lord God, do visit my people in their afflictions."

Heavenly Father was blessing me *in* my afflictions. He helps us when we need it, and I knew everything would work out okay and that I would be able to provide for my family as long as I needed to.

I stayed close to my Father in Heaven and the teachings of the gospel to help me do that. I fasted and prayed for help often. I paid my tithing. I attended the temple weekly. I received priesthood blessings whenever I needed extra strength and comfort. I learned more of the importance of forgiveness as I worked hard to forgive those who were involved in taking the business my husband had spent so many years building.

We were able to continue to run what was left of the business in a way that my income didn't change much in spite of the loss of most of our clients. It met our needs and many of our wants, and my children and I were being blessed because of our choices to remain strong and have faith through this challenge. I was becoming stronger than I had ever thought possible. I *could* do hard things as long as I let Father lead the way. Through the power of the Atonement, I felt the strength I needed every day as a single mother. I am in awe of how the Savior's sacrifice helped me take care of our family in our times of sadness and suffering.

* * *

As I continued to live and grow each day, I felt comfort in reflecting on the conversation Robbie and I had before he died and knowing what he wanted for our children and me. I especially found comfort in knowing I had his blessing to seek companionship in someone else. I had many opportunities to meet new people. It was amazing how many of my friends knew somebody they thought I would enjoy dating. In that time, I learned a lot about myself and what I desired in a future husband.

Some of the men I dated felt threatened by the fact that I had a previous husband I was still madly in love with. I wanted to talk about him and tell stories about funny things he'd said or done. I wanted to share these things so my children would always remember their dad and what a great man he was. I could understand why these men wouldn't want to hear me go on and on about him, but I didn't like that they felt that way. I needed to find a man who wouldn't feel threatened by the memories of my late husband, someone who would honor and respect Robbie's place in our family. But that kind of man would be hard to find, if even possible.

I didn't want to settle for just anyone. I wanted to marry someone who could help bring joy and happiness into our lives again. I knew I needed to choose my next husband carefully. And I needed to be the kind of wife and mother to whom such a man would be attracted, the kind of woman deserving of the great man I was searching for.

* * *

I continued to attend the temple each week and prayed for help and direction in finding the man who would meet my desires and expectations in a husband and a new father for my children.

One day, about three years after my husband's death, I had a friend invite me to dinner with her. Her friend had written an article in a magazine about a couple she had become good friends with during their shared health challenges, and she had the magazine with her. She told me the wife, Kari, had recently passed away and thought it might be a good idea for me to talk to her husband, Evan. She thought I might be able to help him deal with his recent loss in some way and that he might even be someone I could eventually get to know better and date.

As I read their story, I was moved by the amazing journey they had been through. I cried a lot, knowing how much pain he and his children were going through. I told my friend I would be honored to talk to him anytime he needed to, but there was no way a guy like him would be interested in dating me.

First of all, his sweet wife's death had been so recent that I didn't think he would be ready to even consider dating again. Second, he was too good to be true! Tall, handsome, loving, and amazing! She insisted I let her give him my e-mail address "just in case."

I wasn't surprised at all when I didn't hear from him for the next few months. Then one day in church she asked me for my e-mail address again. She said she had given it to him, but he had immediately tossed it. She thought he might be ready to have it again.

Sure enough, he sent me an e-mail within a few days telling me he would be most comfortable conversing only by e-mail as he wasn't ready to date anyone yet. I told him I understood where he was coming from and was just fine with talking this way and helping him cope with his loss in any way I could. He let me know how busy he was with work and taking care of his two sons from a previous marriage, as well as his two-year-old little girl. He said if he didn't e-mail very much, that was why.

I thought it was really cute but could see right through the way he'd set things up to bail as soon as he found out he didn't want to move things along to a phone call or a date. I told him I was fine to take things at *his* pace.

We shared stories back and forth about our families, our interests, and our losses. We found ourselves e-mailing daily, enjoying hearing about how we were both dealing with our new, harder lives, and I fell in love within a few short days.

He wrote his e-mails late at night and set them up to send at eight o'clock each morning. I would wake to the sound of my inbox chime, and my heart would flutter as I read the charming and witty things he had to say. It hadn't been this much fun to wake up each morning in three years! It was such an exciting and nonthreatening way to communicate and get to know each other.

It took him about two weeks to ask me to meet him at a local restaurant. As soon as I saw him I was smitten. He was as wonderful in person as I could have ever dreamed, and at six feet six inches, he was even taller than I had imagined.

We had such a great two-hour conversation that we left with the hopes of seeing each other again the next evening. We either talked on the phone or saw each other every day for the next several weeks and got to know each other quickly. He had all of the qualities and then some that I could have ever hoped for in a man. He was so kind, gentle, charming, loving, witty, good looking, spiritual, thoughtful. . . . The list went on and on. And I felt it was important that he shared my experience. Kari, like Robbie, had told Evan how important it was to her that he find another woman to be madly in love with and to help him take care of and help raise their family, someone who could help keep her memory alive for their daughter. We both wanted a spouse who could help keep our former spouse's memory alive in our home.

As soon as I knew he was the man I would marry, I wanted my kids to meet him. But first I wanted to talk to my oldest son privately to tell him I had met a man I really liked. I prayed to have the Spirit as I told him about Evan. I also prayed that Robbie would be there in spirit to help diminish any anxiety or feelings of betrayal Braxton might have about my being in a relationship with someone other than his dad.

Our conversation shocked me; Braxton was totally accepting of the idea of me marrying again and wanted to know everything about Evan and his children. He asked me what he looked like, how tall he was, what I liked about him, what he did for work, where he lived, where we met, how old his kids were, and what they liked to do. It was so cute how he was interested in all of the little details.

After I answered his questions, he told me he thought I should marry Evan. He hadn't even met him yet, but he already felt like Evan was the right man for us. My prayer had been answered yet again, and I was grateful for another tender mercy.

That night, I invited Evan over to meet my kids. They fell in love with him immediately and wanted to know how soon he could come over again. The next day when Evan came over, my older daughter Alexis, who was ten, bluntly and innocently asked him, "Will you marry my mom?"

He chuckled with that cute smile of his and then replied, "I would love to, but I don't have a ring yet."

Later that night, Alexis, along with my other children, told me they really, really liked him and wanted me to marry him if I wanted to. It brought me so much joy and comfort to know I had my children's approval, and it was easy to see why they gave it. He had so many of the same qualities we loved in my late husband, but there were also different things about his personality we enjoyed.

We were pleasantly surprised to learn it really was possible to love someone again after such a big loss. We didn't have to be out of love or forget about a former spouse or parent to have room in our hearts for another.

* * *

A day or two later, he brought his children over to meet mine. We had a fun pizza dinner together and played games and got to know each other. All of the kids got along really well from the start, and we enjoyed a wonderful evening as new friends and a soon-to-be new family.

We got engaged about two weeks later and were married the following month, the day after Kari's birthday. We had pictures of her and Robbie at our wedding. It was important to us that we honor and recognize them as an integral part of our newly blended family. During our wedding we felt their presence, approval, and great joy.

We have made it a priority to create new traditions while continuing old ones that help us remember Robbie and Kari and honor their place in our family. We try to do all we can to stay connected to Kari's family and friends so Evan's children can have many people in their lives to tell them stories about their mommy. They are such great people to spend time with and to learn from and are good about including us in all they do as well.

For Kari's birthday one year, I took Ellie to visit with many of Kari's dearest friends and each of her sisters. I asked them to share some fun stories and memories of Kari with her sweet little Ellie. I felt that she was old enough to understand what a great woman her mom was and why. We had a lot of fun listening to all of the stories, and I too was grateful to learn more about such an incredible woman because it has helped me be a better mother to Ellie.

* * *

It was so much easier than I ever thought it would be to have room in my heart to love another man the way I love my eternal companion, especially considering all the different things about them. What a tender mercy Heavenly Father has shown me in giving me happiness and love again. I am so grateful that our children have been able to realize this as well. They know they don't have to forget their real dad and mom to be able to accept and love their new dad and mom.

We have been happily married for six and half years now. Blending a family is an incredibly hard thing to do though, and we continually rely on our Father in Heaven to help us know what is best for each of our children and how to help them in the trials they face.

We have found that it is different to step-parent rather than parent your own children. Sometimes I feel like I can never be as good a mom as I know Kari would want me to be to her daughter. It's easy to compare my faults and failures to her many good qualities, but when these feelings of not being good enough get overwhelming, I know I am allowing Satan to play a part in my role as a mother and wife. He would love nothing more than for me to feel like I'm not doing a good enough job and just give up. These are the times I put my concerns and insecurities in a prayer. These are the times I need to draw closer to my Father in Heaven, which in turn helps me draw closer to my husband and our children. I am always a better wife and mother when I include Heavenly Father in my life daily.

Our newly blended family is a work in progress. We are working hard to become closer to each other, and we understand each other more every day. We have all been through a lot of really hard things, but we know our joy will be just as high as our sorrows are low. I am so grateful I get to continue the journey of being a wife and mother. I have so many things I am learning from Evan and from taking care of and nurturing stepchildren. The things I continue to learn here on earth will help me be a better wife and mother in the eternities.

I am striving daily to be the daughter of God I know I can be and to bless the lives of those around me in some small way—the way my life has been blessed by the many angels around me.

Jesus Christ lives. He is my Savior. I am so grateful for the gift the Atonement is in my life and for my testimony, which has brought me through the hard times of life thus far. I know it will continue to do so as hard things continue to come my way, as this is how our testimonies are strengthened. As I keep my covenants, I will be blessed. I am so grateful for each and every tender mercy the Lord offers me in this incredible journey back to live with Him again. Indeed, we can do hard things with God!

Part V: Mental Illness

12
Living with Bipolar Depression and Anxiety
by Elizabeth Harris (name changed)

I AM FIFTY AND BIPOLAR II, which is sometimes diagnosed as an anxiety disorder and sometimes called manic depression. It means that to varying degrees and with some other quirky symptoms, I feel anxiety and depression nearly all the time. I do not have the euphoric highs that are a part of bipolar I. I've tried to think back to the onset of this problem and have realized I can't. It was a part of me even as a very young child—I was a bed-wetter, had chronic stomachaches, and told lies that only the most gullible could possibly believe.

When I was still young, I realized I was different in a negative way. My realization took hold in the fourth grade when I read *The Merchant of Venice* by Shakespeare. The play ends with Shylock, a Jewish moneylender, being legally awarded a pound of flesh as a repayment for a debt, but he isn't allowed to draw any blood in taking his reward. I became obsessed with the ending of the play and dreamed about it over and over. At first I imagined tiny surgical instruments capable of carving out flesh while leaving behind a lacework of minuscule blood vessels, but later I decided it would be better to use lasers. The urgency of the obsession scared me, and I began withdrawing from other people.

I felt some kinship with Shylock and became curious about Jewish people. In the sixth grade, I found my mother's holocaust pictures from World War II. Near the end of the war, she'd been a nurse in a MASH unit at Buchenwald concentration camp, and her pictures of piles of dead prisoners affected me. I began reading holocaust literature and dwelling on death and destruction and the question of what led people to such extremes. In Sunday meetings, I absorbed the concept that we should control our thoughts and keep them spiritual and upbeat, but I failed miserably. So I kept my thoughts to myself.

My obsessions grew to include Jewish history, ornithology, and social causes. I read an eclectic selection of books, and while I read I often felt the Spirit tell me what was moral and what was not. I asked myself questions such as, "Is it better to be the well-fed guard in a concentration camp or one of the people being starved and tortured?" Often during this kind of internal questioning, I felt the Spirit whispering, and that became an important foundation for my later understanding of the gospel.

Among my peers, I developed a reputation for being weird. It wasn't just because of my obsession with offbeat subjects. When in school, I was either withdrawn and moody or aggressive. I was the know-it-all kid with my hand in the air, ranting on about issues other teenage girls didn't care about. I was smart enough to do well in my classes, but I struggled to maintain the concentration needed to do homework or maintain a normal social demeanor.

School was a disaster, and my church and family relationships fared even worse. My relationships with kids at church impacted the rest of my social life. One girl in my ward became the impetus behind the bullying that took place at school. As a result, she became one of my strongest fixations.

At home, my mother looked at my features and saw her abusive father. Because of my similarities to my grandfather, my mother took her anger out on me, and when I felt threatened by her, I retaliated with a "take no prisoners" approach. We were left with a mutually abusive relationship, and I cultivated a seething hatred for just about everybody. In the midst of this turmoil, my mother was called as stake Relief Society president and held the position until after I went to college. Her long service in that calling had a profound impact on both of us.

Because we lived in a rural area and her calling required her to be gone for long periods of time, I was often either home alone or in the car, tagging along to a stake function. When we traveled, I sat in angry silence, hugging my door, while she lectured me on the truthfulness of the gospel. I hated her for it because even though our relationship seemed beyond repair, I knew every word she told me was true. I despised feeling spiritually sensitive when she talked to me.

She told me stories about people from all over the stake—of a man who had seen a dead relative and been led to a genealogical discovery, of women who were abused but used the Spirit to deal with their problems, of people who did not obey the commandments, and of her own life and troubles and the answers she got to her prayers.

I felt that I had something to prove, so I refused to speak on these trips, which gave her hours and hours to tell stories. Despite my efforts, the stories sank in, along with the strengths of all the characters in books I read, and I began to value strength in women.

I was admitted to Brigham Young University toward the end of my junior year in high school. It seemed like a miracle. In one fell swoop, I escaped my high school, ward, and family. I had a penchant for religion classes and a dream of someday teaching Old Testament for BYU–Jerusalem. I developed strong relationships with some of my roommates, and my life seemed to be moving in an upward direction. But every time I visited home, I fell into the same old pattern of anger and hatred.

* * *

Two things happened during those college years that had a profound effect on helping me change.

First, I learned that the Lord would give me answers to questions. My roommate Barb began questioning the meaning of *glory*, and I started noticing the varied instances of light in the scriptures. We talked about these subjects during our freshman year and began to realize they formed a relationship. One night, as we were discussing Doctrine and Covenants 88, the subject opened up to us in a series of revelations. Barb would say something, and it would trigger a wave of understanding, and then I would say something to her, and she would have the same experience. I began feeling better than I could ever remember feeling—hopeful and positive and stronger. Over the next several years, I learned more about the topic, and the revelations kept coming. For a few years, the veil became very thin for me. I learned that I could pray about anything— evolution, polygamy, race, my homework. If I studied and my mind was ready, the Lord would help me understand all of these things.

The other thing that happened was that I took a philosophy class from Terry Warner. The gist of what I learned was that our emotions are rooted in our perceptions. When we change our perception of a situation, our emotions change as well. It was a gripping realization to see that my anger was a way of justifying my part in twisted relationships.

The class homework involved analyzing ourselves for self-deceptions, and just like in those long car rides with my mother, I knew what was true, and I rendered myself mute. I didn't hand in a single paper the whole semester, which meant that to get rid of my F I had to retake the class.

Spending eight months on the subject of self-deception and anger was enough time for me to develop new habits and a plan for dealing with my anger.

* * *

When I was old enough to get married, I had some decisions to make. I was alternately forceful or withdrawn, not particularly pretty, and not sweet in the way nice Mormon girls were sweet. I wasn't sure I wanted to give up on marriage completely, but it seemed unlikely that I would find someone, and I had never dated anyone I could imagine spending my life with. Nonetheless, I was lonely and wanted my life to have meaning, so I decided to serve a mission. When I went to my bishop to ask him about my serving a mission, he told me to go on a date and make some guy feel like a man. In context, I believe he wanted me to have a positive social experience and then see if I still wanted to go on a mission.

I wasn't a girl who got a date every weekend, so I had a sizable problem. When an old family home evening brother, Ted, asked my roommate Barb to go out with him, I told him she was engaged but that I was free. He seemed unexcited but politely invited me over to watch a movie. We barely talked that night, and I doubt that he felt any manlier when I left, but I felt I had tried to do as the bishop had asked.

Oddly enough, that night while saying my prayers, I had the quiet impression that I should be willing to marry Ted if he chose to continue a relationship. I was caught completely off guard since my reason for dating him was to pass off a requirement for a mission. While I liked him, our date was without doubt the most awkward I had ever experienced. Besides, the feeling that I was to marry him was not an explosion of understanding or peace but a request I didn't understand at all. I couldn't fathom why the Lord would want me to marry someone who was so obviously uninterested in me.

In spite of the difficulties, I didn't feel like I could turn my back on that prompting. Ted and I dated for two years. In spite of the fact that we didn't become close, he had been told by bishops that he needed to marry. We each had our problems. I had clear problems with my mood and productivity, and he had a sexual addiction and gender issues. We also both came from abusive families, and because of our parents' early deaths, we both struggled to resolve childhood issues. On top of all that, we both acknowledged we didn't love each other, but still we felt compelled to keep moving forward. Three months after his mother sewed my wedding dress, Ted asked me to marry him. As soon as we became husband and wife, the gates of hell opened wide.

Marriage stressed both of us to the breaking point. I spent most of the first ten years sleeping or staring out of windows, my mind racing in what I now call "blender brain." When I felt extreme anxiety, my thoughts became a montage of brief images, song fragments, stressful conversations, and suicidal thoughts. Blender brain rendered me almost incapable of carrying out tasks. Dirty dishes went untouched for days, and I tried to hide how completely dysfunctional I had become. I still had a testimony, but I vacillated between the vague hope that the Lord would somehow rescue me and the clear realization that I was too depressed to maintain any stable level of spirituality.

For years I'd heard that if I would just exercise and read my scriptures consistently, I would get over depression, but I was incapable of doing anything consistently. Taking care of my home, when I did do it, and fulfilling my Church callings took every bit of energy I had, not to mention dealing with my husband, who escaped into a fantasy world of sexual addiction and gender issues.

Ted and I had children, and during the kids' grade-school years, I realized that if I was going to raise them better than I had been raised, I needed to act fast and get over my problems. I went to a psychiatric nurse practitioner for my treatment of depression just as Prozac and the new class of antidepressants hit the market. She tried them all on me, but unfortunately, giving antidepressants to a bipolar person feeds their mania, or in my case, my anxiety.

The year or so I spent experimenting with psychiatric medication was the worst of my life.

For months I cried so much that I was thirsty all the time. One day I put on a brunch for the mothers of my youngest daughter, Linzi's, preschool class (Linzi is mentally disabled), and I cried through the brunch. When someone asked what was wrong, I told them I had allergies.

* * *

Extreme anxiety made everything seem like a threat, and my impulsive reactions were often severe. One afternoon I had Linzi in her car seat next to me for the drive into town. Her disability prolonged the baby stage of sticking fingers into eyes and ears, and as she reached over to stick her finger in my ear, I balled up my fist and swung it as hard as I could toward her face, catching myself just as my fist lightly touched the tip of her nose. She seemed a little surprised, but it scared me.

During this period, I helped my son with his homework through the bathroom door so I wouldn't hurt him for making mistakes. I saw strange things, like the yarn in our bath mat growing and shadow people moving in the periphery of my vision. I moved from psychiatrist to psychiatrist and through a few different counselors, but I couldn't find a psychiatrist or counseling that provided solutions instead of more problems, and I worried about what I might do while trying all the different psychiatric medications.

* * *

The Church was a mixed blessing for me. On the one hand, I was always blessed with good, strong friends who supported me, but I also felt guilty that I wasn't more put together for each of them. Visiting teaching companions in particular provided support I didn't get from anywhere else. As we drove those country roads, my companions offered understanding and sincere love and acceptance. One day, one of them drove me around for miles while I stared out the window, too overcome to say anything at all. But I appreciated the time she gave me.

Another Church blessing was teaching classes. I loved that feeling of unity when the Spirit moved all of the class together or the extra help the Spirit gave in understanding the scriptures.

Because I am bipolar, people sometimes have a hard time dealing with me. I am more intense and less feminine than other women. I speak up more often in classes, more frankly, and get derailed on tangents more often, but then, overwhelmed by that, I avoid people. I often mess up dates and times. People who try to control me find me particularly difficult to tolerate because I am usually oblivious until I see their fury. My initial reaction is surprise, but that gives way to reciprocal anger, and it becomes as hard for me to deal with them as it is for them to deal with me.

When the situation gets too intense, I work my anger plan. I prayerfully contemplate whichever person is upset with me and then make an honest appraisal of what I did to spark their anger. I understand that they are angry with me as a justification for their own self-deception, and as I change my perspective, my anger dissipates. I find that the same few people tend to get angry with me repeatedly, but as I practice my plan, I react less and less toward them, and my feelings gradually become more loving and understanding.

* * *

As the years passed and my husband and I both sought solutions for chronic emotional and behavioral problems, I gradually became more and more cynical about bishops' abilities or desires to help. When I was first married, I saw bishops as all-powerful men who could, if they only would, force my spouse into taking care of his problems. Many of them looked at me and thought that if I were a better person, Ted would improve as well. Sometimes I felt angry with them and had to work my anger plan until I could change my perspective, but because of these struggles, I came to realize that bishops couldn't solve problems for us; they can only guide us. Instead of relying only on them, I focused on praying for guidance to solve my own problems.

That guidance came gradually, line upon line. In the beginning, it was the Holy Ghost whispering to try a hormone supplement, then He guided me to take Linzi to support group. While there, I learned about food allergies, therapies, and different kinds of doctors. I began experimenting and discovered the world of alternative medicine, which led me to some quacks as well as to some amazing practitioners who took the time to listen to and analyze my problems. With the Spirit's help, I was able to discern the dangerous practices and the time and money wasters and begin making the lifestyle changes that led to a substantial difference in my mental health.

Today I still have some mental health problems, and I'm sometimes overcome by blender brain, but most days I function almost normally. I walk each morning, take handfuls of supplements, and follow a strict diet. Most people don't realize I have mental health issues unless I tell them. My children are young adults now, have testimonies, and are generally responsible. My youngest attends a special-needs school. I eventually made it through a bachelor's degree and then a master's, held down jobs, and am now working on a doctoral degree. I function in my Church callings and no longer experience the social angst I did when I was young. Ted and I are still married. We struggle much less with our relationship, but it's a slow, quiet struggle without the extremes that characterized us twenty years ago. I am mostly at peace.

* * *

My experiences with mental illness have taught me to take nothing for granted. I've learned that the brain is a critical part of the body and that our general health has a huge impact on our mental health. Those in turn have an impact on our ability to be self-disciplined and act in the gospel. I've learned that people are meant to take on challenges and that when we allow ourselves to stagnate or give up our agency, depression is the result. I've learned that Heavenly Father loves me, but I will still have some hard trials. I can accept that.

Some mornings I wake up and my mind is a black, swirling mess. If I can push through and feel love or make a prayerful plea, the Holy Ghost intercedes, and for three or four powerful seconds, I am filled with His presence. It differs from His influencing me in that it is more direct and physically overpowering. It changes my mental state on a more fundamental level than by giving me thoughts or ideas. It took me some time to realize this was the Holy Ghost, but He helps me function when I am most needy. Because of the Spirit, I have learned more empathy for the weird, the awkward, the disabled, and the lowly, and also for the beautiful, the smart, and the composed. In some ways we all live in different worlds, and I understand that it is just as hard for me to see into someone else's world as it is for them to see into mine. We are all fighting a hard fight, but the Lord gives us the insight we need to fight on the same team.

If there is one thing I hold on to, it is the memory of the night Barb and I shared learning about light. It provided a foundation that helped me connect all the principles of the gospel with an understanding of and a feeling for the nature of Jesus Christ. Whatever spiritual endurance I have has its roots in that night. Barb has since left the Church and, at one point, asked me to leave as well. I couldn't do it. Despite all my upheaval and erratic relationships, Jesus Christ is real to me and is a constant. I take Him very personally, and I believe He takes me that way as well.

13

Spouse's Mental Illness: You're the One Who's Bipolar, So How Come I'm Going Crazy?

by Laryssa Waldron

YEARS AGO, MY FRIEND JENNIFER[27] and I were returning home from a road trip. En route, we were pulled over twice for speeding. The first time, we left with a warning, the second time with a ticket. After that, Jennifer watched her speed and drove more carefully. Suddenly, and with no signs or warnings, a deer slammed into the windshield on the driver's side, bounced off the car, and fell dead at the side of the road. We were in total shock.

Due to the circumstances of the evening, we chose to keep going home. Miraculously, the windshield's tempered glass held together, but it made driving difficult for my friend. She could see only by leaning over to the middle and depending on her mirrors and my help and guidance.

While I was preparing to write this essay, that experience came forcibly to mind. As I have met with other women who are in similar situations, I have felt a tangible heaviness when we have revealed that our spouses are bipolar. We don't need to swap stories. We know, understand, and deeply feel what the other has gone through in trying to drive to our heavenly home as passengers in a car whose driver has to proceed with a broken windshield. Other caregivers may watch from a safe distance and may gain understanding and insight, but they are not in the car. They do not have to entrust their entire welfare and the welfare of the children in the backseat to the hands of a person who is unable to completely see the road ahead with accurate vision.

* * *

Bryan Waldron has always been a force. As a young man, he was outgoing, athletic, attractive, a good student, and spiritual. When he turned nineteen,

---

27 Name changed.

he was excited to serve a mission in Bolivia. About a year into his mission, he was sent home because he began to exhibit strange behavior. He was diagnosed with "a nervous breakdown" by the elders and a "brief reactive psychosis" by the doctors.

Bryan was in the right place doing the right thing when he was hit. It was by no fault of his own, no sin, no being in the wrong place at the wrong time—just like the deer slamming into the car though we were going the speed limit and being safe.

* * *

Bryan was home for about a year, never released and often going on splits with the elders, before they figured out what to do with him. He said he was coming out of a session in the LA Temple when he felt a distinct impression that he needed to finish his mission. When he pursued that prompting, he was assigned to work in California until he received his new call to the New York, New York South Mission. There he served for almost another year but was sent home again with mental problems—this time to be diagnosed as bipolar disease (i.e. manic depression).

Bryan's patriarchal blessing stated twice that he would have the mental, physical, and spiritual strength to be a husband and father. When he received that blessing before his mission, his family thought the mental part was a little odd, but they didn't take much notice of it. After the experiences of his mission, he was absolutely certain God knew him and had a plan for him.

Bryan had other blessings long before we met (on several occasions by different priesthood holders) that also promised him he would be healed of the disease.

* * *

A friend once told me that when I got married I would take on the trials of my spouse. What he said basically meant that if my husband needed growing and stretching, I would be part of that test too, like it or not. That was counsel I thought about deeply as I yearned for marriage. I wanted to be the BYU stereotype. I wanted to get married young and have a dozen kids. Yet I believed our loving Heavenly Father would bless my life with instructions and guidance if I asked for it, and I have always been one to ask and follow a path of obedience.

My path took me on adventures ranging from Eastern Europe to the U.S. Army to a rewarding career to an eventual master's degree. My life was full, though part of me still yearned for a family of my own; it wasn't until I was finally content with the prospect of being single that my future husband knocked on my door for a blind date.

Bryan was a typical Waldron man. He saw me, decided I was the one, and practically proposed on the first date. He was vivacious and friendly, and I loved being around him. Soon after we started dating, he told me he had a chemical imbalance and that he just had to take his pills regularly and he was fine. He simply glossed over it, making it sound as easy as curing a headache by taking an aspirin.

I had met people with mental illness, but they seemed as normal to me as anything. I had no real experience with it, and everyone I talked to said the same thing—all they had to do was keep taking those meds and everything would be well.

Though Bryan got more serious about me, I wasn't really interested in more than a friendship until I found out about his mission—he had served for over three years, in three different missions, under four different mission presidents. That was what made me take a second look at Bryan. I had served a mission in Bulgaria. I knew how difficult missionary work and life was, and for him to go back out and serve by choice when he technically had an honorable release was interesting to me. It showed that he had a love for the Lord. It showed that he knew how to follow spiritual promptings. It showed humility, bravery, and an ability to sacrifice and put the Lord's will first. I wanted to get to know him better.

* * *

During our courtship, I received divine guidance. It was the same guidance I had received previously. It had never led me astray, and the thing was, I really loved Bryan. I enjoyed his personality and our friendship. Plus, everything was easy, not like dating had been for me in the past. It was like being in a maze, but instead of hitting dead ends, the corridors opened one after another until the end magically appeared. All I had to do was walk.

I made the decision to drive home with him, cracked windshield and all. I climbed into the car knowing his trial would be mine, and I fully intended to help him make it home as long as he was willing to try as well.

As time passed, I set up a few guidelines for myself. These were mine, and mine alone, because I knew everyone was different and needed to follow the Holy Ghost in whatever their circumstances. The first guideline was that if he was ever physically abusive to me or our children, I would leave in that moment and never look back. The second was that if he didn't take his pills (intentionally allowing himself to go manic), I would divorce him. The third was that if he was lazy and didn't try to work or tried to keep me from living the gospel, I would separate from him for a period until I knew whether or not he was willing to try to work things out.

* * *

Anyone who gets married quickly knows they are putting a lot of faith in the other person. It was on the honeymoon that I started to notice some odd and quirky behavior, but Bryan was taking his meds, so I was sure everything would be okay. I assumed that most marriages had struggles the first year, and ours certainly had some ups and downs, though we were able to cope. I had a good job, we had a great income and stability, and I loved being with my new husband.

We soon began to plan for a family, deciding to have Bryan finish school and be the breadwinner while I stayed home with the kids. We knew things would be a little tight with money if I quit my job, but again, it felt like the right thing to do.

The summer right before our first wedding anniversary, Bryan began to have trouble sleeping at night; it was as if his body was going right over those wonder pills that were supposed to keep everything together, and after a few nights of not sleeping, Bryan began to talk nonstop. His mind was full of racing thoughts, and his speech was nonsensical—a giant stream of random consciousness with no end in sight. I had never experienced anything like it before. Our doctor was out of town, and we were unable to get help or contact his office. We went to a new doctor who helped by prescribing a new miracle drug. As Bryan came down from the high, I decided we should hold off on trying for a baby for a while so I could help my husband.

Then I got a very real and distinct impression from the Holy Spirit that it was my choice to have a baby or not and that if I did get pregnant, it would be a decision I would never regret—not one day of my life. But the Spirit gave me that choice with a caveat—that those feelings of joy and assurance would come *after* the delivery. The reassurance that I would never regret the decision felt sure and solid, so I got pregnant with our first child, and we moved into married housing at BYU in order to be well positioned when the baby came.

That pregnancy was when all the strings that held our life together broke loose.

* * *

Bryan was in a deep depression for five months of the pregnancy, and the medication he was on played with the chemicals in his brain, causing a mix of both racing thoughts and depression, which was not a typical combination for a bipolar person. It was like the worst of both worlds combined.

Depressed Bryan was so difficult to be around. It was sad to see his vivacious and fun-loving spirit crushed. The joy and happiness of life drained out of him. The parts of his personality I enjoyed the most were stripped down to a shell of a man who walked slowly behind, unable to engage in the world around him. I tried to have joy in the baby coming, but Bryan never wanted to discuss it; he wouldn't even watch the ultrasound video. On top of that, he didn't want to be with people, had a knee operation, and cycled through jobs. While I dealt with my own pregnancy hormones and sickness, I was Bryan's caretaker.

During a really low point in Bryan's depression, we were sitting in the car, and he began to talk about life having no meaning; it was then that I realized how truly sick he was.

Before that moment, I'd had a vision of what we as a couple would someday become. I'd made a checklist in my precollege days: home, perfect job, five children, Church callings, and college degrees—everything the young eighteen-year-old Laurel in me had dreamed up. We were trying to meet those goals and had moved twice during the first five months of the pregnancy to try and help Bryan succeed, but at that moment, the reality of who he was swept my mind free of any lists, glory, or success.

I bowed my head in prayer and begged Father in Heaven to help my husband heal. I gave up all of my ambition. I didn't care if I lived in an apartment for the rest of my life, if he never made it through school, or ever held down a job. I simply wanted him to be okay.

* * *

At the end of my seventh month of pregnancy, I called the doctor in desperation and asked if he could please help Bryan. The doctor told me to put him into a psych ward to help stabilize him, with the intent to sort out the medications. In one day, he fooled the doctors and was released, happy and carefree. I figured he was fine. But he wasn't. He was high flying; had been up the entire night, though he had pretended to be asleep; and within a few hours I knew they had released Manic Bryan into the world. I spent an entire week of my eighth month of pregnancy trying to help him come down from the mania.

Manic Bryan was a nightmare! He held several faces, each one with its own unique twist. One of those faces was just plain crazy. When he came out of the hospital, he shaved his hair off at 3:00 a.m. The next morning, I was trying to understand why he looked so weird and finally realized he had shaved off his eyebrows as well. He also did things like fill out tithing slips, one for every week—for the next year.

Another face of mania was an out-of-control face. Often, people on a manic high are promiscuous or go on spending sprees. Thankfully, Bryan was the latter. One night I woke up at four in the morning, and Bryan wasn't in bed. He had gone to a grocery store and bought $300 worth of size-five diapers for the new baby. We returned the diapers to the store. Later, I reflected on the fact that even in irrational times, Bryan didn't spend money on items destructive in nature (e.g., drugs, pornography, and alcohol). Usually, his spending sprees involved buying things for the family, things we had talked about buying but were unable to afford at the time. Though the situation was difficult, it was comforting to know that the very core of his spirit, even when he wasn't in his right mind, was good.

There was another face to Manic Bryan, one that was absolutely mean. There was no other way to describe it—just a mean, argumentative, verbally abusive, and cruel human being. It was difficult because I knew this face was covered under the Atonement—that he was inculpable of some of the actions and behaviors—but even with that knowledge, it was difficult to live with.

He constantly insulted me, yelled at me, and embarrassed me. If we went to the store, he would fill the cart with unnecessary items and then berate me in front of total strangers when I tried to tell him we couldn't afford $200 of specialty cheeses. The yelling and name-calling would continue until I finally decided the cheeses were easier to deal with than the emotional beating.

He tried reading a book while driving, and when I told him to quit because it was unsafe, he yelled at me and tried to keep doing it. In desperation, I got out of the car at a stoplight until he agreed to either put the book down or allow me to drive. Then I got an earful about how I was being mean because, after all, I wanted him to read more, so why was I being a jerk and not allowing him to do that?

To others, Bryan was goofy and acted strangely. To me, he was manipulative and full of rage. I knew this was Bryan in the disease and that he was not like that normally. However, in those moments, I felt like an emotionally battered woman.

To keep my sanity and our finances somewhat together, I started dropping him off at the library, unleashing him on the unsuspecting library attendees. He had cards to three different library systems and would go in for an hour or so at a time. I would sit in the car and try to sleep or at least be alone in my own head for a few moments. When he was finished, he would come out with thirty books he planned to read that night.

We'd also go to movies, where it was relatively dark and quiet.

At one point, I dropped Bryan off somewhere and went to my parents' house. I could feel the baby inside my womb shaking, and I knew it was from the stress I had been carrying. I asked my brother for a blessing because I needed to find a way to calm the baby down. In that blessing, I was promised that from that moment, her emotions and mine would no longer be connected. The shaking ended immediately, and I felt so blessed that though I could do nothing for Bryan, my prayers for our baby were efficacious.

Everything totally exhausted me. At night, my sleep was constantly interrupted from both the pregnancy and Bryan's sporadic sleep patterns. I would wake up at all hours to find him up doing something or other. I was also working full time and had to muster the energy for that load, on top of surviving what Bryan was undertaking when I returned home. And when Bryan decided we should move for the third time, when I was eight months pregnant, I was so tired that I decided to just go with it.

* * *

Finally, Bryan began to sleep. He came down off his high, and for two wonderful weeks, he took care of me. He rubbed my feet, cooked, cleaned, unpacked, and made sure my comfort was his first priority. It was amazing.

Then one night, about a week before my due date, I woke at 4:00 a.m. to find Bryan at the computer. Somehow, he was back in full manic mode and had spent $1,000 on Amazon products we were unable to return. The craziness had returned, but this time Bryan wouldn't go to bed when I asked him to. He wanted to stay up on the high by intentionally not taking his pills. Every decision he made seemed deliberate, and he was angrier and meaner than ever before.

I could go no further in the marriage. I got in the car, having made the decision to leave my husband. I now understood why people divorced, and I was ready to go and never look back. I got ten miles down the road when the Holy Ghost intervened. He asked me to go back to Bryan and reminded me of my temple covenants. "You promised me you would take care of this man," was the direct thought that came into my mind. To me, it was like an Abrahamic trial. No human could have said that to me. I knew this communication was from Father in Heaven because I knew His voice. I never would have done it for any other being. I turned the car around and went back to Bryan. I did it for God, because I loved Him, and for no other reason.

The moment I made that decision, I felt hands on my head (though I was alone in the car), and from then on I was filled with a different power and strength to carry on. I was given specific and direct revelation and promises that there was purpose in my choice that the future would reveal. I came to know that Bryan needed to use his agency as well, and in prayer, the Spirit and I came up with the second rule. I firmly began to tell Bryan I would leave him if he didn't choose to get it together.

We went to see a new doctor soon after that, and when we walked into his office, he saw my belly and cheerfully said, "You know, one in four of your children will be bipolar."

I almost walked right out of the office, but something told me to stay and listen to what the man had to say. He told me Bryan needed sleep. He said that as long as Bryan was getting at least seven hours of sleep a night, he would never go manic again. It was like throwing a life preserver to a drowning woman.

I had just been given hope and a new direction—if I had to knock Bryan out with medication, he would get that sleep! That night, I told Bryan that if he didn't take his meds and go to sleep he would not be allowed to see our baby be born. I told him I would call the police and have him barred from the hospital. He told me it was the meanest thing I had ever said to him. It may have been, but I was drained in every possible way—physically, mentally, emotionally, and spiritually. I could not deal with labor and mania together.

Bryan took the pills, and a few days before we had our precious little girl, Bryan came down off his manic high. After we brought baby Jillian home, I lay awake in bed listening to both of them sleeping, praying that they wouldn't wake.

The next night, Bryan began scratching his back on the doorpost and told me it really itched. When he took off his shirt, his back was black and blue as if he had been beaten with a whip. He went to the ER, and we found out he was allergic to his medication. I called his doctor in an absolute panic. He told me I sounded like I was the one going manic. Maybe I was. I just couldn't take another mania on top of a new baby.

After the doctor gave us a prescription that acted like a tranquilizer for a charging elephant, we spent the weekend at my in-laws' house. Bryan and I both slept while his mother held our baby, brought her in for feedings, and then took her away to cuddle her so I could sleep again. That act of kindness saved my life.

Shortly afterward, Bryan got a full-time job with benefits, and the new doctor prescribed a set of meds that were the absolute perfect solution for him. They worked with his body chemistry, they put him to sleep four hours after he took them every night, and they have worked for the past nine years.

* * *

After we had Jillian, I got a strong impression that I needed to stay with Bryan and let him provide. I was to write, work part time, and be a wife and a mommy.

That impression was completely contradictory to logic. I had the college degrees; Bryan hadn't finished his bachelor's, so it made perfect sense for me to work full time and support us. But the Holy Spirit was prompting me to do things differently.

I had the impression time and time again that I was to put Bryan in charge of getting full-time employment with health benefits while going to school. Could someone who was mentally ill deal with such heavy burdens? And yet, what would it be like if I didn't follow what the Spirit was so clearly directing me to do? What would Bryan be like if I just left him to continue to cycle? Left him floundering? What kind of a man would he be? What kind of a family life would we have? Would the pressure of being a father help him with the healing?

I decided to follow the Spirit.

There was a joke I heard once about a golfer. Every Saturday for years, this man and his friends went golfing from eight in the morning to twelve o'clock in the afternoon. One day he didn't come home at noon, and his wife began to worry. Finally, at two in the afternoon, the man came through the door.

"What happened?" the wife asked with obvious concern.

"Oh, Charlie went and had a heart attack on the first hole, so after that it took forever! It became one long game of hit the ball, drag Charlie, hit the ball, drag Charlie."

I figured I could either pull ahead, dragging my husband behind me when he was obviously in serious need of care, or I could go slowly.

With Bryan as the breadwinner, our progress has been in a state of two steps forward and one step back. When we seem to advance, we immediately fall back, so our progression at times seems minuscule.

I spent the next few months obsessing about Bryan's sleep, and each morning when he woke up in his right mind, I began to breathe a little easier. When our baby was a few months old, Bryan lost his job and then found a new one. I took a part-time job as an adjunct professor of English, which has given me the opportunity to help support Bryan as the provider but has left most of the burden for financial provisions and medical benefits on his shoulders. The part-time job allowed me to be with my daughter most of the time.

That winter, when Jillian was six months old, we got in a horrific car accident (we hit black ice on the freeway and slammed into the concrete barrier twice). Miraculously, we all made it out safely, but two days later Bryan lost his job again. As an adjunct professor, I had several months a year that I didn't get paid. We were headed straight into my dry period. We had no car, no income, and it was Christmas—yet I was still alive, still breathing, and still continuing to exist.

That was when I realized everything in my life could be taken from me, and when the next morning came, I still had to get up and go on. Because life still continued when the tangible things of the world crumbled away, I had to figure out who I would be when I had nothing. Would I still have my happy nature? Would I still be optimistic about life? Would I still have the strength to try to care for Bryan? What kind of home life would I give our child? Would I still live the gospel, or would I "punish" God for the trials by leaving Him?

I decided to stay with the gospel after that accident, and it became a Christmas of miracles. Each week, money came in (anonymous gifts, kind friends, even a check from an overpaid credit card bill—figure that one out!)—just enough to survive another week.

That December, Bryan began to get serious about being a provider and worked a bunch of menial jobs to help bring home as much money as he could. He often worked a day job or picked up temp jobs—anything he could find to bring money home. It gave me more ability to trust him. We began to be blessed little by little, and whenever we desperately needed it, answers and help came.

* * *

We moved two more times, Bryan went through more jobs, and he worked on schooling for the next two years. By Jillian's second birthday, Bryan was two classes away from getting his bachelor's degree from BYU and had landed a good job. Then we felt like it was time to try for another child, and I got pregnant. Suddenly, Bryan began to fall into a depression again. He lost fifty pounds and started having problems at work.

After twelve weeks, I had a miscarriage. I was at the brink of my own sanity. We were living from paycheck to paycheck, wondering whether or not we'd have the money to pay rent, put food on the table, or pay the power bill, and the creditors from Bryan's manic days were still calling. I worried constantly about Bryan's sleep and that he would go into another manic cycle after this depression. I worried that he would just quit his job without another to take its place. Living in such chaos and upheaval, always having to be strong and keep it all together, had taken a toll. I told Bryan that because of the miscarriage, it was my turn to be depressed. For some reason, having me to care for pulled him back out of the sadness.

When my parents invited us to move into their basement apartment, I began to feel some of the stability I had been craving for the past five years. At least I knew the owners weren't going to evict us. A month after the miscarriage and within weeks of moving, I felt a strong impression that Jillian needed a sibling and that by choosing to bring another child into the world, we would all be blessed. I got pregnant again.

When I was six months pregnant with our second child, Bryan was in trouble at work. He didn't like the job and wasn't motivated to go, and his tardiness was endangering his position and our health benefits (you know, those that covered his illness and my pregnancy). I, in extreme panic, had been getting up, trying to get him out of bed, choosing his clothes, motivating him with choice language, scraping the car windows when there was frost and snow, and altogether exhausting myself in order to get him where he needed to be. Our bishop sent us to a therapist.

The counselor asked me why I was doing all of it.

Seriously? I thought, *His choices affect my life and our family's life!*

I wanted to scream at the man.

Then the therapist simply stated that I could do nothing about Bryan's agency; I could only do something about my own. If Bryan made certain decisions that affected me in a negative way, I had every right to make my own decisions, and there was nothing he could do about it.

For the second time in our marriage, I threatened Bryan. He needed to add to the marriage. He could be the stay-at-home-dad or be the provider. Either way, he had to work. He could choose, but falling down on the job was no longer an option. If he wanted to be the provider, I would allow him the opportunity, but if he kept failing, we would separate until I could see an improvement in his ability to work.

* * *

When I was seven months pregnant, Bryan quit his job with benefits.

I was ready to take my agency and leave. But a miracle kept us together. An overwhelming calm and peace came over me—it was pure grace. I knew everything would be taken care of. Bryan got a temp job, which gave us temporary benefits, and I had our second girl, Sofia. Then Bryan got a full-time job, which he held for four years.

He is learning to be the provider, though being mentally ill continues to be tricky. For example, we've had to be quite creative in maintaining insurance benefits, yet we've kept continuous coverage for nine years now. It's been miraculous. I once heard something about allowing the Provider of the Universe to teach your husband to provide. It is always amazing to me that Bryan has continued to get job after job. Lately, we have seen some stability. Bryan's meds, our home, and Bryan's job have been steady and constant. I feel more confident about my Father in Heaven, my husband, and myself.

"I have seen his ways, and will heal him: I will lead him also, and restore comforts unto him and to his mourners."[28]

* * *

Over the last few years, I have been noticing changes in Bryan. Awhile ago, I felt like a newlywed finding out who my husband was for the first time. I've been able to look at Bryan's little quirks and say, "Oh, that's *you,*

---

28 Isaiah 57:18.

not the disease." I didn't know Bryan before the windshield was cracked. I think of that as a blessing. His family has said, "The old Bryan is back again." Hearing that has given both of us a lot of delight.

I wonder now if the promised healing in Bryan's case was a gradual one. After a while I came to the conclusion that maybe it didn't mean the mental illness would leave completely but that we would get so good at managing it that it would be as if he were healed. We still have rough spots and rocky times—points when his logic isn't completely sound or when we have to walk a razor's edge between a manic or depressed episode—but we live according to a strict schedule to make sure he gets dinner, meds, and bed at specific times, and it works. I have to have the availability to be present for him and our daughters at all times, which has made friendships, callings, and work difficult, but it's getting easier to live with.

* * *

The following are some of the things I've learned that have helped me move forward as we try to make it safely to our heavenly home. It's much easier to see these principles when not in survival mode, and it is a great blessing that I have had some time between experience and writing.

Remember the Atonement and allow it to be a part of the relationship

As I've been learning to trust in Bryan's abilities, I have had to learn to look at him through the lens of the Savior and His magnificent Atonement. I have learned to forgive repeatedly. I have learned to rely on the Savior's gifts to allow me to stay married.

There were times when I truly hated my husband. I couldn't stand the sight of him. I wanted to say to the universe, "Hey, mine's broken. Do over!" But the things that made me crazy about Bryan were covered by the Savior's phenomenal gift. Any mistakes and misuses of agency would and could be forgiven as long as Bryan was trying to move forward.

I prayed and prayed for charity. I prayed to love and care for my husband again. I constantly "pray unto the Father with all the energy of heart, that [I] may be filled with this love."[29] Slowly, steadily, I have found love for him again. I sincerely enjoy being around him. He is a kind and loving man, and I find joy in our home life and the things we have been able to accomplish together. I hope I will continue to find deeper and deeper love and unity with him as we work on making our family eternal.

---

29 Moroni 7:48.

Focus on the positives

I have had to learn to look at what Bryan brings to the relationship, not at what I want him to bring. That is difficult. I wanted us to have stimulating, intellectual conversations. We don't. We talk a lot and enjoy each other's company, but I have to turn to personal study and conversations with others to get intellectual fulfillment. It's discouraging at times, but in order to continue to build our marriage, I have had to constantly remind myself that Bryan may not give me what I expect but he gives me what I need.

He makes me laugh, is a great date, is fantastic at parties, loves others, is loyal, cleans, makes the most amazing BLT, does laundry, does the bills, creates amazingly detailed systems of organization, makes phone calls, returns stuff to the store, buys things for me when I am too cheap to buy them for myself, is an amazing cheerleader, is my protector, trusts my judgment, and loves me intensely. Together we make a pretty good whole.

Allow others to help

It has been difficult to accept help. I feel bad that I have sometimes used the lion's share of others' resources. I try to be keenly aware of when I have put too much of a burden on someone else's shoulders. It's much easier to be the giver than the receiver. All I know is that I couldn't have survived without our friends and family, and I hope one day I can give some of what I have received back.

Show grace to the Lord

During the fall of 2011, Bryan's bosses, who had so much patience with him, put him on part-time status. I won't go into all the details, but it meant we lost benefits for six months. So we had to be creative again because Bryan couldn't afford to lose his health benefits with his mental illness. The medication that keeps him sane costs $350 a month without insurance—and that's just one of his medications.

As we faced future uncertainty again, I realized it was my turn to show the Lord some grace under pressure. He had always shown us the way through as we faced the same issues over and over again. "[We'd] proved Him in days that are past."[30] It was now my turn to go calmly to Him for direction and answers instead of freaking out about the situation. He provided those answers, we stayed covered, and now we have insurance again through Bryan's work. Daily, we still live on the edge of falling apart,

---

30 "We Thank Thee, O God, for a Prophet," *Hymns*, no. 19.

but we constantly have the promise, and now the track record, of divine help and guidance.

Follow the direction of the Holy Ghost, even when others don't agree

One would think I should just get a job. It makes sense for me to provide. We certainly fall under "the exception to the rule" category, but every time I have tried to take over, things have fallen apart with Bryan. One summer I took a consulting job that earned an extra income. Bryan began to miss work, and his kind employers docked his pay for the missed days rather than firing him. When we did the math, Bryan's missed income was the exact amount I had added. We hadn't progressed one bit.

I want him to "drive the car," even with its broken windshield. So we've had to go slow. We live with my folks. I don't get paid for three months of the year. We've gone to the Church and our families for help. We pay off debt when we can. And we pray often and see the lilies of the field in our lives. It's been difficult for me to receive help, but I've seen a side of life that has taught me about the great blessing of welfare and has given me an overwhelming amount of compassion.

Use your agency to do, and you will be happy and fulfilled

As I have allowed Bryan to move forward in the driver's seat, I have done some fun and amazing things as well. Every time we've faced an issue, I have been prompted to sit down and write or grade papers or read to my children. In desperate times, when I wanted to force the situation to bend to my puny will, I have found that the only thing I have any control over is my own agency. I've learned to throw my time and attention into the things I can do—work, nurture my family, and write. I have been strangely fulfilled through my effort in these areas. Choosing to focus on that rather than the worry of what is happening or what could happen has been a blessing.

My job as an English professor has led me to the niche of technical writing, which I love. As a teacher, I find that each new student opens my knowledge of the world. They write on subjects about which they are passionate, and I have received an education right along with them in fields I would never have studied but am fascinated by. From my students, I've learned about nanotechnology, string theory, engineering, excavation, computer technology, pharmacology, nursing, nondestructive testing, and land surveying.

My part-time job permits me to spend most of my time with the girls. It is amazing to have time to actually spend being a mother, which seems to be a rarer thing these days, and I count it a miraculous blessing. We read, swim, craft, cook, and clean, among other things. I take such delight in the time and friendships I am building with my beautiful girls.

In my free time, when the girls are napping or at school or the house is quiet, I have been able to write, which is something I have always wanted to do. I've written two books, created three blogs, and written a number of articles. I've started a small publishing company, which has published five books, with more in the works. I love writing almost as much as I love teaching. In it I've found the ability to feel the guidance of the Spirit and enjoy the spark of imagination that turns into the process of creation. Other demands on my time have made my writing move at a glacial speed, but I've already learned through my marriage how to go at a much slower pace, and so the sluggish process is not only bearable but enjoyable.

I've also seen the power of healing through creation. I kept my sanity during difficult times by following the Spirit's guidance to write. After finishing this essay, my relationship with Bryan has been more enriched. Somehow, the process of finally writing down the experience allowed me to place it behind me and gave me insight into where we are now compared to where we have been. I love and appreciate my husband more than ever before.

Keep your eye on the eternities

Bryan gets frustrated because his younger brothers have houses and we don't. I have to keep reminding him that we are on a slower track than they are. Then I remind him of the things he's been able to do since he was diagnosed with bipolar disease: He went back out and finished his mission. He's become a successful husband and father. He serves in the Church. He hasn't had a full-blown manic episode in nine years. He's held down a job with benefits for many years. He finished his bachelor's degree as well as a master's degree. It's an absolute miracle that he's able to be as stable as he is with such a debilitating disease.

No, marriage isn't perfect bliss for us. It's been challenging; however, I feel so proud of what we, with God's help, have been able to accomplish as a married couple in eleven short years. I am amazed at the woman I've become and the man my husband is. I look forward to what the future holds, with trepidation at times but mostly with great hope that things will get better. I'm sure we'll keep following the pattern of two steps forward, one step back—but at least we're moving forward.

I look forward to one day seeing Bryan behind the veil, when his wind-shield is fixed. I look forward to the "same sociality which exists among us here . . . [existing] among us there, only it will be coupled with eternal glory, which glory we do not now enjoy."[31] There, through the Savior's miraculous gifts, I will clearly see who I am married to.

---

31 D&C 130:2.

Part VI: Alone but Not Lonely

14
Singlehood

by Betsy Ferguson

* * *

HE WOULD BE WONDERFUL! WE would meet at BYU. After graduation I would teach elementary school for a few years as he finished his education. We would have a house filled with children. Our lives would be busy with family, Church, community, friends, and each other. He would have a successful career, enabling us to build our savings, retire at a young-ish age, and we would dedicate ourselves to service in the Church. It was a great plan. It was even a plan with righteous desires. But it was my plan, not the Lord's plan for me.

* * *

In Psalms 27:14, we read, "Wait on the Lord: be of good courage, and he shall strengthen thine heart: wait, I say, on the Lord." I had a bishop who noted that it is often the sisters who do the waiting—waiting for a missionary, waiting for a proposal, waiting to be pregnant, waiting for nine long months of pregnancy to end. It is even our right and privilege to wait upon the Lord. However, not all waiting comes to a conclusion in this life. Even so, the Lord's promises are sure. If we keep our covenants, He will not withhold any blessings from us. And when we receive our desires, we will truly cherish them.

I like to think of waiting on the Lord in two different ways: The first is in the sense of being patient with His timing. I've always found the phrase "in the due time of the Lord" (D&C 138:56) to be such an ambiguous measure of time. There is no such hour on the clock or date on the calendar. It's impossible to schedule anything that takes place in the Lord's due time on my iPhone. Waiting on the Lord certainly demands that I develop patience and faith.

But there's a second way to think of this phrase that gives me greater direction. I see myself as a servant of the Lord, waiting upon Him and doing His will. While I've never worked as a waitress, I have been waited upon by many who have served with varying dispositions and abilities. It gives me cause to reflect upon my own behavior as a servant waiting on my Lord. Do I deserve a good tip? Everything depends on *how* I *wait* upon the Lord *while* I *wait* upon the Lord.

Among those of us waiting for the blessing of marriage in our lives, our experiences vary vastly. Yes, there are some similar happenings and shared emotions, but our paths are as individual as we are. As I attempt to share some thoughts about my journey, I know my experience is unique to me, and others may feel differently than I do. But perhaps for those of us traveling this road in life alone, sharing with others how we navigate the roadblocks and detours may give us a sense of companionship and shared strength to make the journey.

* * *

As I began to recognize that marriage and family might not arrive on the course and in the time frame I had in mind, I confronted the challenges I shared with so many in my same situation. I felt unsure of how to prepare for the future—and exactly which future I was to prepare for.

In the early years, my stage in life impacted my planning only in the smallest of ways. For example, I found myself delaying purchases. I would hear myself say, "You shouldn't buy a stereo system. Guys always buy those. Whoever you marry will already have one." I remember looking at kitchen plastic ware and thinking I shouldn't invest in real silverware because that was the kind of thing people gave as wedding gifts. Eventually I recognized the folly in postponing purchasing items I would use in the present. Had I not changed my mindset, my life would be void of so many things, and I certainly would have nothing in which to store my leftover lasagna.

Making purchases, of course, became even more worrisome when I finally decided to buy my first home. Would it be in a good location for meeting people? Did I buy something that suited my needs now, or should it provide sufficient space for a potential marriage and family? By the time I purchased my second home, I was considering myriad possibilities and attempting to buy a home suited to any number of unknown futures. How could I possibly make a thirty-year financial commitment to a property when I couldn't see what my future might hold only six months from now? I purchased a large home with a rental space that would offer me financial support and the security of having others in the home. I hoped it would also serve as a potential living space if I were to care for my mother someday. If I were to marry a widower or divorcé with children, the six bedrooms would hopefully meet our needs. If I opted to take in foster children, the bedrooms would also be necessary. Or maybe when I chose to serve a mission, the home would enable me to have someone live in the rental space and care for the place without my having to move from it. So many unknowns.

* * *

Certainly, the more weighty decisions were those related to education, career, and professional pursuits. While I didn't wish to focus my life on a career, I also didn't wish to live on the streets, so I had no choice but to become financially self-sufficient. From the time of my earliest memories, I had wanted to be a teacher. My love for children and my passion for working with them left little doubt that elementary school would be the place for me. Besides, I felt it would help prepare me to mother my own children. I would work while seeking out the man of my dreams.

But how does a person who should be a member of Perfectionistic Workaholics Anonymous keep from becoming so consumed with the day-to-day demands of the job that she doesn't neglect the important goal of marriage and family? It is a lingering issue. As I have pursued advanced degrees, I have sometimes been hesitant to avail myself of opportunities that were conditional upon future years of employment or other constraints that might be difficult to fulfill if my marital status ever changed. Even as I began my doctoral program, I questioned whether I could further my temporal pursuits and maintain a proper focus on things of eternal significance.

So how does one plan and prepare for a long-term future of being single while simultaneously maintaining an open mind, an open heart, and an open schedule that permits the possibility of marriage? My answer was to surrender. I surrendered my plan. I surrendered the control. I surrendered my will. Early on I surrendered it all to a perfectly loving and perfectly knowledgeable Father in Heaven. My plans were good and would provide a happy life, but I had to trust in and have faith that the plan of an all-knowing and loving Father would be far superior to my own. His plan for me would bring not only a lifetime of happiness but an eternity of joy. I've learned that my responsibility is to seek to know and do His will in all things. My plan now is simple—I try to do what the Lord would have me do. This still entails making decisions, but I trust that the Lord will help me know what is right or wrong for me. And while it often means a step into the darkness and working out most of the details on my own, I can clearly sense the hand of the Lord guiding me when I am trying to do His will.

* * *

"So why aren't you married yet?"

You'd think after all these years I wouldn't be caught off guard by that question, but it still seems to startle me. How should I answer it? I've experimented with a number of different retorts. Sometimes I answer, "Because I haven't found anyone with a high enough tolerance for pain." Other times I simply say, "Nobody wants me." If I can cause my lower lip to tremble just a bit while saying it, this tends to make the individual regret asking the question, which I sometimes think they should.

Of course, another favorite question is, "Don't you *want* to get married?"

While I find this one equally irritating, it also provokes my thoughts. *Do* I want to get married? The obvious and simple answer is a resounding and emphatic "Yes!" However, after several decades have passed with that goal unmet, I have naturally begun to build up some barriers to protect my heart. It logically follows that if I want something less, the pain of not having it will ease. So maybe I shouldn't let myself want marriage so much. Indeed, we are counseled to seek marriage but to not make it the sole focus of our energies. But not making it my sole focus is different from not wanting it as much.

Many people will understand that when you long for something and are denied it for what seems to be an extended period of time, it is natural to tell yourself that whatever you're unable to attain probably isn't that important or worthwhile anyway. But marriage to a worthy priesthood holder for time and all eternity *is* both important and worthwhile. And I have learned that the Lord, while not wishing me to make the goal to be married the epicenter of my world, does want me to nurture that desire. Whenever I have, for a time, let that desire slip, excluded marriage from my prayers, or told myself that because I might not get married I should probably just let it go, the Lord has brought it back to my remembrance as a righteous desire. During one of these times, I attended a ward temple night when we participated in a sealing session. I was there with several happy couples from my ward, and although acutely aware of my single status, I was eager to serve as a proxy in the sealing ordinance of my great-grandparents. During the session, the Spirit reaffirmed to me both the eternal significance and the divine beauty of the sealing covenant, and the Lord told me very clearly that it was vitally important that I want this for myself—that I want it with all my heart, even if it was not to be mine at the time. In that moment, with the clarity that sometimes accompanies spiritual communication in the temple, I could fully understand that these blessings were eternal and that when they were afforded me, it would be for eternity and that this period of waiting would seem but a small moment. In truth, this time of waiting and wanting would make the blessing of marriage that much sweeter.

* * *

Have you ever had that dream in which you awake from an accident with amnesia and find you have no memory of the last several years of your life? There are times I think I would love to simply wake up and find myself married. Okay, so it would be a bit of a shock to the system, and I'd have lost the beautiful memories of meeting, courtship, and falling in love, but let's face it, after blind date number 2,357, amnesia doesn't really sound so bad after all.

Often, people who married in their early twenties will say, "It must be so fun to go out on dates!" But while I may have a great time on a date, I must confess that I don't find dating fun.

It may seem unfortunate to those of us whose time in the dating pool is measured in decades, but dating is still considered the socially conventional means to courtship and marriage. So because the issue is forced upon me, I have the ever-present question of whom to date. Because I work in an elementary school setting, it naturally follows that the vast majority of the males I meet are under the age of twelve and are still waiting for their voices to change. My ward is filled with wonderful people who wear wedding rings, so that's not a dating Mecca. Some suggest that I avail myself of the single-adult activities, but I feel like I've paid my dues in that area.

As a child of a single parent, I began attending single-adult activities at a young age. By the time I was six years old, I had received a special invitation to the annual recognition dinner, where I was awarded the certificate for best conversationalist. I was a member of a single's ward when I was still of Primary age, and after all those years in the singles programs of the Church, I felt it my right to swear off all singles activities and stop going.

It was only when I was serving on the stake council in a stake preparing for a mass transition of 150 single adults from the BYU singles wards to our family wards that I made an unwilling return to the world of organized Church singles. The stake council had asked for my thoughts and opinions on the transition, and I had willingly obliged . . . for which the stake presidency asked me to attend meetings and activities to assist in the transition process over the next several months.

This meant I had to attend the singles activities once again. For the first couple of months, I managed to survive and even met some fabulous individuals. However, at one Sunday singles fireside, three handsome young men—who happened to be three of my former third-grade students—approached me. After that, I asked for permission to once again fade from the singles scene.

* * *

Given all of the above and my aversion to anything like unto online dating, I was left to the mercy of the blind date. And as much as I really don't relish the notion of another blind date, I still feel obligated to participate. If I'm going to spend time on my knees asking the Lord for the opportunity to be married, how can I turn away dating opportunities?

It would actually be quite easy to turn them away. It's easy to recognize when someone wants to set me up on a blind date. There's a certain hesitation in their voice, their eyes don't meet mine, and they use an unnatural pause before they say something to the effect of, "I don't know how you feel about it, but . . ."

To be honest, sometimes I don't know how I feel about it. I've had a blind date enter my home and, upon seeing my picture of the Savior above the mantel, say, "I usually don't like pictures of Jesus in a house, but that one's not so bad." While working on my master's degree, I was set up with a man who had no job, no schooling, and no real plans for either; he lived in his parents' basement and liked to fish. I also went out with a nice man who owned multiple Star Trek costumes he wore to conventions. Yes, he could speak Klingon. A kind ward member wanted to set me up with a friend of hers from work. When we spoke on the phone, I could tell that the man was trying to learn my birthday. I thought that perhaps he was attempting to determine my age, but I was wrong. "I used to live my life by the Spirit," he explained, "but I got burned too often. So now I follow the Chinese Zodiac." We didn't go out after all.

It's possible that I'm too picky, but I hope that's not the case. I really have very few requests for those who wish to set me up. They should actually know me and the other side of the date and have some reason to believe we might get along with one another beyond the fact that we are both single. As for the man they are setting me up with, he must be stalwart in the gospel and have some kind of active occupation or scholarly pursuit. I also appreciate it if the person is closer to my age than my mother's. That's it. I've given no caveats regarding widowers, divorcés, or any other such thing.

And yet I'm still single, so perhaps my expectations are still too high. I don't know. However, I feel that the only thing to do is press forward. So I continue to meet people when I can, accept blind dates, and keep myself open to other potential dating opportunities to create experiences in which I may meet other wonderful people known simply as "singles."

* * *

Life is good. As I look around me, I am grateful for the opportunities I have been afforded. I recognize how abundantly blessed I have been, and I am happy. But regularly tasting of the goodness of God does not mean I never have moments of discouragement or heartache. I am often alone, but rarely am I lonely. However, when that loneliness does come, it is often accompanied by a deep ache and a longing for the companionship of someone with whom I can share everything. Someone who knows my story so that when I talk about the day's happenings, his eyes widen because he immediately understands all of the implications without my having to explain them to him. Someone who allows me to carry his burdens and sorrows alongside him and who will help me shoulder my own. Someone who will lovingly help me improve upon my faults and make me a better person. Someone to help make life's important decisions. Someone with whom I can share a knowing glance. Someone who laughs with me when no one else gets it because "you just had to be there"—because he was there and is there, sharing and building a lifetime of memories with me one day at a time. When I see friends who have that person, and I recognize that I don't, my heart aches just a little.

However, that ache does not prevent my heart from sharing in others' joy. Just because I do not yet have certain blessings in my life does not mean I cannot rejoice for those who do. I am thrilled when I learn of a friend's engagement. I'll admit that when the upcoming marriage is one of my former fifth-grade students, I sometimes twinge with thoughts of "Really?" yet I'm always so excited for them and so happy to be included in the occasion. I also celebrate the birth of every precious baby who comes into the lives of those around me. Admittedly, there is sadness beyond words that I may never have children of my own, but I thrill in the addition of new life to my friends' families and am so very grateful for those who let me share in their joy.

* * *

One day, after a Church meeting, a loving ward member apologized to me for speaking about the happiness she experiences with her husband and children. I almost didn't know how to respond. I know that there are those for whom discussions of this sort cause pain, but that is not my experience. I believe the Lord feels tremendous joy in families, and if we will permit Him to do so, He can replace any feelings of heartache, jealousy, or unfairness with the same amount of joy. We can choose to fill the void in our hearts with bitterness or with the love of God.

That is not to say that I have never felt pain at something someone has said or done or that in my own weakness I have never taken offense. Fortunately, it is rare that any offense is intended, and through the Lord's help, I am able to regain perspective.

I am so blessed to have many wonderful people who will let me hold their babies and play with their young children at church. One particular day, I sat in Sunday School next to a brother with a baby boy far too young for nursery. After a few minutes, I asked to hold the baby and was enjoying having this young boy on my lap when his mother entered the class. She immediately said, "Oh, I can take him if he's bothering you."

While he was in no way bothering me, the repeated gestures of this mother clearly communicated that she wanted to hold her baby, so I gently returned him to his mother. She intended no harm, but my heart cried out, "If you only knew how much it meant to have him in my arms for just a few moments! He's one of four children and yours forever. My arms are empty. Could you not have possibly shared him for a few minutes more?" At the close of the meetings that day, I went home and cried for hours.

I have on several occasions had parents apologize to me for their children's disruptive behavior at church. I always try to let them know I am grateful for parents who faithfully come to church week after week and do their best. These parents know they will likely miss much of the meeting while picking up the spilled Cheerios or walking out to the foyer once again with the toddler whose nap time sacrament meeting happens to interrupt. Although I do my best to help at any given time, I, for the most part, am free to focus on the speaker and the message of the meeting. I understand that they often wish they could experience a meeting without dispensing Goldfish crackers and crayons, but I would give much for the privilege of having to haul around a diaper bag of supplies for my children. Though we may desire aspects of others' situations, the Lord has given each of us specific and personally designed experiences. The more faith I have in His plan for me, the less I will mourn what is not mine and the greater joy I can find in the life I live now and in the lives of those around me.

* * *

Unless I'm in an irksome mood, it amuses me whenever someone asks, "Without a family, what do you do with all your free time?"

Free time?

Well, without a spouse to share the responsibilities, my "free time" is spent working a full-time job, teaching night classes, running a small business, landlording two properties, working on my doctorate, shopping for groceries, cleaning the house, cooking the meals, repairing the car, filing the taxes, doing the laundry, calling the plumber, mowing the lawn (or worse, shoveling the snow), paying the bills, attending my caucus meetings, serving in Young Women, and fulfilling the myriad other life responsibilities that must be completed on a daily, weekly, monthly, or yearly basis. The unimaginable for me would be to try to do all of this alone *and* care for children. God bless the single parent!

While I don't believe I have more free time than others, I do feel I have a certain degree of flexibility not afforded to those who are married and/or have children. I do not have anyone with whom to coordinate the use of the car, nor do I have anyone to call when dinner's running late. I am the master of my schedule, and there is a certain degree of freedom in that. However, as with most singles, I think I'd gladly sacrifice some of the flexibility in order to have someone there who misses me when I am not at home.

One benefit this flexibility has offered me is travel. I have been fortunate to travel around the world, and my life has been enriched as I have made friends around the globe. Much of this travel has been to provide service, but as we all know, anything we may give in service is returned to us one hundredfold. For example, I have traveled six summers to Ghana, West Africa, to volunteer and have met many of the finest people I know who have taught me much through their examples and goodness. I have gained such a tremendous appreciation of all I am blessed with (not the least of which is clean, running water and dependable electricity) and have felt an overwhelming desire to spend my days in the service of my Lord, knowing that where much is given, much is required. I certainly have been given much.

The Lord expects me to utilize my time well and be engaged in many good causes. I try to consistently challenge myself to learn, to grow, and to become what the Lord would have me be. I find that my time is well spent if I am furthering my education or in some way developing talents and desirable qualities or serving those around me. And while I sometimes feel tired and wish to withdraw from the business of life and retreat to the tranquil world of my own home, I fear stagnation. I do not wish to miss the opportunities the Lord has so amply blessed me with in my life because I spend my time wishing for the opportunities He hasn't.

* * *

On occasion, various acquaintances have said, "Well, since you don't have your own children, at least you get to be the favorite aunt!" This isn't exactly consoling, because the unfortunate fact is that being both single and an only child, I have no nieces and nephews. While I may not yet have the roles of wife, mother, or even aunt, though, I feel a great responsibility to magnify the roles I currently do hold. I have been blessed with an amazing mother, so I recognize that I need to work on improving myself as a daughter. I need to become the best cousin and niece possible. I have many wonderful family members who enrich my life, and I understand that while I wait for the Lord to bless me with other family roles, I must demonstrate my best in the family stewardships He has given me now.

I'll confess that I have a fear that there might be unintended and undesirable consequences of living alone. When one does not have to participate in the daily give-and-take of life at home, I believe it's possible to become selfish or self-centered. The simple acts of negotiating and sharing can be lost without daily practice. Although none of us enjoys having our faults brought to our notice, it is a blessing to live in a family and to be surrounded by those who help us to recognize our weaknesses and help us grow. I sometimes worry that without others in my home to keep me in check, I might develop and allow to become ingrained in me negative qualities and poor habits. I rely upon the many friends with whom I am so greatly blessed to hold up that metaphoric mirror. I don't wish to become the "crazy old cat lady."

Another fear I have is that others will not consider what I am as enough—my single status will be all they see—so I feel the need to show them that I am more and that I am of value even though I am not married. I recognize this as my own foolishness and pride. As children of our Father in Heaven, each of us is of divine heritage and infinite worth. My need to prove myself or to "show my résumé" is a human frailty. Only when I turn to my Father in Heaven on my knees and seek to know my standing before Him can those fears, uncertainties, and preoccupations with the approval of others be assuaged. In reality, only His approval matters. And if I go to my loving Father with an open heart, He is able to bring peace to my soul about the things that are right in my life and make clear the ways in which I must next focus my energies to improve and become the daughter He wishes me to be.

* * *

Although there is much in my life that at times seems confusing and my future often feels so uncertain, when I pause to adjust my perspective, life regains its clarity. The answer to all of my many fears and concerns— indeed, the remedy for all life's challenges—is simple: live the gospel in its fulness. How blessed we are to have the revealed truths of the gospel of Jesus Christ in our lives! Within the principles and doctrines of the restored gospel are found the answers for life's difficulties. When the Lord said His way was easy, I believe He meant His gospel eases the way for us. It eases our questions about the purposes of this life and what we are to do. It eases our way by guiding us in how we should live. It eases our burdens as we understand there is a purpose for our trials and that a loving Savior is there to help sustain us through them. His burden is light because He strengthens us and increases our capacities, enabling us to bear all that is required of us and allowing us to find joy in doing so.

I have learned that being active in His gospel means I must also be active in His Church. The organization of the Lord's kingdom here on earth provides many opportunities and blessings. Being single and living away from family, I have come to understand the great boon of a ward family. I have been sustained and supported by the service of ward members and have received the blessings of giving service as well. Accepting callings I know are beyond my capacity is daunting, but I have felt the sustaining hand of the Lord guiding me to do my part in building His kingdom. Many of my most treasured friendships began as I served with fellow ward members, and my life has been deeply enriched by their influence and examples. These friendships have extended as we have moved far beyond the ward boundaries, and I feel certain that many will continue to bless my life throughout eternity.

* * *

Although the gospel is universally applicable, as a single individual in a family-oriented Church, I have sometimes struggled with the question, "How does this apply to me?"

Once, when attending a Saturday adult session of stake conference, I felt myself becoming the slightest bit resentful. The theme of the meeting and, therefore, every talk given, addressed strengthening marriages. My very large ward at the time was comprised nearly entirely of young married couples, yet as I looked around the congregation, with the exception of the bishopric and their wives and one or two other couples, I could not see the members of my ward. I'm ashamed to say that I momentarily entertained the self-righteous thought, *Here I am trying to do my best to attend my meetings, and it doesn't even apply to me. They have the blessing of marriage that I so want, and yet they're not here, where they should be.* Fortunately, the Lord softened my heart and gently reminded me of the admonition I so often give myself: "Do not say this does not apply to me, but, rather, ask *in what way* it applies to me." In doing so, I have yet to find a lesson, talk, or gospel principle that does not have applicability in my life.

And as I strive to live those principles, they bring peace and joy to my life. When I hold family home evening—studying *Preach My Gospel,* watching general conference, reading Church literature, or working to once again earn my Personal Progress with my young women—I am strengthened. When I work to have more meaningful prayer—through the use of a prayer journal, expressing greater gratitude, or focusing on listening while still on my knees—I find myself closer to Deity.

A wise priesthood leader once suggested that I study the Book of Mormon in relation to a calling I was given. I studied and marked a new copy of the Book of Mormon, seeking inspiration from the Lord to direct me in my given stewardship. I have since utilized this practice with many callings, including my calling as a member of a family. When I study the Book of Mormon, the promised blessings come. And whether I am serving as an ordinance worker or worshiping as a patron, temple attendance greatly enriches all aspects of my life.

It is a tremendous thing to know there is a great plan of happiness and that I have a part in that plan. The eternal perspective the gospel gives me enables me to see beyond the seeming limitations of my current situation into the expansive hope of eternity and the fulfillment of all the Lord's promises. I may, at present, be without the blessings of the sealing covenants with either parents or spouse, but I trust in a perfectly just, perfectly knowing, perfectly loving Father in Heaven and in His plan for me. I know it is a personal plan designed specifically for me and for my eternal salvation. My *personal* plan of happiness. And in choosing to live His plan for me, I can indeed find joy in each of my todays, my tomorrows, and my happily ever after.

15
Unexpected Loneliness in the East
by Linn Allen

ONE THING I LOVED ABOUT our home in Boston was that it was quiet and peaceful. Many nights, I would walk out to the back porch, sit in the dark, and look at the stars, feeling safe and happy and close to my Heavenly Father. But one fall night, about three years ago, as I stood on our porch, the dark and the quiet felt suffocating and isolating, and it intensified the feeling that my heart was breaking.

As I stood sobbing so hard that I had to use the deck railing for support, I wondered if it was too much, if this would be the one thing I could not overcome, if there just might be exceptions to the promise that we will never be given more than we can handle. I clutched our telephone in my hand and stared at it with tears streaming down my face, believing at the time that I had just had my last verbal communication with my parents for the next several years. A sadness filled my heart, the depth of which I had never felt before, and I sincerely wondered if things would ever change.

Did I know that many have been through much worse? Absolutely. Did I know that compared to a terminal illness, a physical deformity, a straying child, a severe handicap, or the death of someone you loved with all of your heart this was low on the devastation list? I did. But did it also feel like the last three years of losing a connection and a closeness to almost everyone who mattered in this life, coupled with having to say good-bye to my parents that night, was too much for me to bear? Without question.

And to be honest, I needed to cry. I needed to grieve. And I needed to be heartbroken. Because soon enough I would take a deep breath, wipe my tears away, and walk into my house. I would see my husband working on his laptop on the couch, and his look of concern and sadness for me would bring me back to what really mattered: he had been the one who had *always* been there for me, and that was never going to change. And it was an absolute honor and privilege to be his wife.

Afterward, I would walk into each of my children's rooms, see them asleep, and be reminded of a belief I feel as deeply as anything I have ever known: I was put on this earth to be a mother. And gratefully, in my case, that involved being a mother to my children here and now. Nothing that had happened to me in the past three years, including that night, could change that. But if I let it, it could change me for good or bad.

I chose good.

For my husband, for my children, and for my God, because I had come to know intimately what I had been taught from the time I was a little girl: I am a daughter of God, my Savior's Atonement is completely and wholly enough, and in our trials and extremities we come to know our God in the way He intended us to know Him. That privilege is worth *anything* we have to go through.

* * *

In August 2008, my husband and I, our four children, and our small truck of possessions moved from our beloved San Diego to a small town outside of Boston. We had moved more than our share (nine times, to be exact), and we were no stranger to new homes, new neighbors, new friends, new schools, and new wards. Some moves involved ridiculously easy adjustments. Others took some time—several months—to feel grounded and happy and at home. Because of that, I never expected an adjustment of many years.

New England is wonderful. New England is different. The people are private. I knew this, or at least had been told, before we moved there. I found the information interesting, but anyone who knows me knows *shy* doesn't describe me in any way. *Loud* and *crazy* are more accurate. So, gratefully, making friends has never been a problem for me, and the ridiculous number of Christmas cards we send out is an example of this fact. So because creating friendships is something I come by easily, secretly I was pretty positive I could win our New England neighbors over. It had always happened in the past, and I had no doubt I could help it happen in the future.

Turns out, this loud and crazy lady didn't stand a chance.

* * *

When we moved to Massachusetts, we didn't see another neighbor for several days. I don't mean we didn't meet a neighbor, I mean we didn't *see* a neighbor for several days. I was beginning to think the homes were decorations. I considered walking up their driveways to make sure they were 3D. But eventually the neighbors came outside, we chatted, they went back inside, and that was pretty much the end of it. There were times when they were so kind and thoughtful and reached out, and it has meant the world to us (snowblowing our driveway one winter day when my husband was out of the country on one of his business trips, a neighbor bringing over a gift after our fifth baby was born, and a sweet neighbor talking to me several times over the fence that divides our yards). Yet the reality of it was that our life there was just quiet. And isolated. And quiet.

Much like our neighbors, our Boston ward was kind to us, and our love for them was tremendous. They always had smiles for us on Sunday, they brought us meals for two whole weeks when I was on bed rest, and they always asked how we were doing. But both the culture of the area and the geographical boundaries (a forty-minute drive) made for an isolated situation even within our Church family.

So, as you can see, life was lonely in Boston. And it could be very hard. Over and over again I grabbed my courage and reached out to those around me—in the neighborhood, in the ward, in our children's school—you name it, I tried it. Sometimes it went well, but ultimately, I hadn't been there since birth, or people were just too private for me to break through.

* * *

When our family had lived in Massachusetts for six weeks, I was called as the Relief Society president. (It was one of the few times in my life I have ever been speechless.) I spent the next two years experiencing some of the most wonderful and the most difficult moments of my life. I was not prepared to love the women in our ward as deeply as I did or to feel so fiercely protective of them. I was not prepared to hear stories that still make me teary just to think about. I was not prepared to be devastated to the deepest part of my heart when things happened to them or because of them and they suffered. I was not prepared to care as much as I did and to feel so lonely myself at the same time. I was not prepared to handle so many serious problems and not have anyone to turn to, to talk to, or to help me navigate through them. And I was not prepared for how the Lord would sustain me, love me, and show me over and over again how much He loves His daughters.

It was not long after I had been called as Relief Society president, still feeling new and vulnerable, that I had an experience with several of my family members that left me feeling broken for the next several months. Without going into details that don't matter, I felt like I had completely lost the love, support, and communication of most of my family members. There are no words for the devastation I felt. To be honest, there are no words for the sadness I still feel at times. Some of those relationships have not completely mended, and I have had to work through some feelings I've needed to ask for forgiveness for, from anger to hurt to justification for my feelings to all sorts of emotions. There was nothing like family members turning against me to not only break my heart and make me feel lonely but to also make me wonder what kind of a person I could be that the people who are supposed to love me the most did not. It was a deeper, more hurtful loneliness than anything I have experienced.

Several months after the experience with my family, a small group of women who had been inviting me to their fun activities every few weeks stopped their invitations. I later learned that one of them did not like that I was becoming friends with her friends and felt like I, as a newcomer, needed to stay away. There was no question that her actions stung, and it hurt that the other women had gone along with her wishes. Those outings were some of the few times I felt like I could get out to visit and talk and laugh with other women and moms. It was hard, and it felt so strange to be dealing with something that seemed so childish at this stage in life. But gratefully, it was not nearly as difficult as it might have been had I not been learning and growing so much with my calling and familial issues.

Six weeks after I was released as Relief Society president, my sweet husband was called as the bishop of our ward. (It was one of the many times in his life he has been speechless.) My husband is incredible. He is good to the core. He serves with every bit of his heart and soul. And I wouldn't want it any other way. Yet, through the years that he was bishop, I learned more intimately an extension of the lesson I learned for two years as Relief Society president: at times, there is an almost unbearable loneliness to leadership.

Oh, how the Lord blesses us and constantly lets us know He is there and is mindful of us. But it can still be difficult. With my husband's calling, I found that my already quiet and isolated life became that much more quiet and isolated. Bishops are incredibly mindful of the confidences with which they are entrusted—as they should be. My husband was beyond mindful of that trust and was extremely careful about not sharing *anything* even remotely close to what he should not. And because of that (and I happen to know from speaking to others in our same situation that we are not alone in this), it sometimes became a subconscious habit to keep from sharing other things as well. In addition, he was gone a lot, which was exactly how it was for anyone with a time-consuming calling in the Church. And I spent quite a bit of time handling our family life on my own—not because my husband didn't want to be involved or didn't do *everything* in his power to be a part of everything he could, but because that is the other side of the stick you pick up when you accept the calling of bishop.

Because I spent so much time handling life on my own, I too got into the habit of not sharing as much as I should. We both had to work at and watch carefully to make sure our loneliness during that season in our life was kept to a minimum and that we shared and relied on each other as often as possible.

* * *

A few months after my husband was called to be bishop, I received a phone call from my mom. Her voice sounded different as soon as she started speaking, and I soon found out why. A member of the First Presidency had called my parents in and had asked if they would accept a calling as the president and matron of a temple six thousand miles away. With tears in their eyes and with humble hearts, they accepted. My mom was calling to let me know.

I don't know if I have ever been as excited for someone as I was for my parents in that moment. I immediately started to cry and had such a strong feeling that this was where they were needed. I felt so grateful to have parents who would choose the right over the easy. I told my mom so and let her go so she could share the news with other family members. I got off the phone and felt giddy to my very core.

And then it hit me. My parents were leaving . . . for three years . . . and our communication would be incredibly limited. They were leaving, and I would be giving birth to our fifth baby just days after they left. I started to sob.

I love my parents fiercely. They are not perfect, but I have come to understand with each passing year that they are perfect for me. My mom and I are incredibly close, and before they left, we talked often. And while

I didn't talk to my dad as often as my mom, we were also very close. At the time, I felt like I was about to lose all of that and that some of the last people I felt I could turn to and talk to and get advice from, who loved me no matter what, were leaving me. Losing that support became a great trial in my life. But as anyone who has been through trials can testify, I have learned truths that have changed who I am and have changed my relationship with my Father in Heaven and my Savior, Jesus Christ.

* * *

So what have I learned from this trial of loneliness? First, while there is no guarantee that those around me will always be there or respond how I would like, ultimately, I am never alone because my Savior is *always* there. There is no loneliness so dark, deep, and heavy that it could *ever* keep Him away. No matter how much I have struggled with the unexpected loneliness of not having close friends and friendships, I have my Savior. And if I feel removed from Him, it is not His doing—it is my sole responsibility.

In a 2009 general conference talk, Elder Jeffrey R. Holland said, "Trumpeted from the summit of Calvary is the truth that we will never be left alone nor unaided, even if sometimes we may feel that we are."[32] With all of my heart, I know and have experienced that what Elder Holland said is true. We are never alone. In spite of any suffering, any grief, any loss, or any loneliness, He is there. And it is our privilege to do whatever is necessary to go to Him.

* * *

A related lesson came to me from time spent in the scriptures. Alma 17:10 has become one of my favorite scriptures, and I've read it more times than I can count, though during difficult times I read it with new eyes: "And it came to pass that the Lord did visit them with his Spirit, and said unto them: Be comforted. And they were comforted."

During a time of particular struggle, something new stood out to me. I knew the Lord had visited the sons of Mosiah with His Spirit. I knew that after the Holy Ghost had visited them, the sons of Mosiah were told to be comforted. But what touched my heart in a way that I was not expecting was that they *were* comforted.

---

32 "None Were with Him," *Ensign*, May 2009.

They didn't turn to the Lord and say, "Thanks, but what we're going through is really hard, so we just want to wallow for a while. Did we mention it's really hard?" They didn't say, "Thanks, but we could use a little more than comfort here. How about an easier way to get around the wilderness and some extra food so we don't go hungry?" No, *they were comforted.* They chose to receive the Lord's peace.

The Lord comforts us more often than we realize. Once I started to focus on *my* responsibility to receive that comfort, I began to recognize the tender mercies that happened over and over again as I traveled this unexpected and sometimes painful path of loneliness.

* * *

In addition, my trials have also taught me to not give in to the temptation to feel unworthy. I have learned that I have everything I need to be happy right now. We all do. But at certain times in our lives, we may feel unworthy of that happiness. Though this unworthiness can come from sin, there is another perceived unworthiness that comes from feeling like we are not enough. The lack of close family and friends can influence how we view our worth if we are not careful. It can make us believe we are not enough and that if we were of value, those around us, especially those who are supposed to love us the most, would recognize that.

And that is absolutely not true.

We are worth it. Every single one of us. And we are enough exactly as we are right now. Every single one of us. Our Father, the God of Heaven, and our Savior, the Creator of the universe, love us wholly and completely just as we are at this moment. It does not matter how alone or unworthy we feel—none of that has to do with our worth or our goodness or our value before our Father in Heaven.

Of course, this life affords us the chance to do better and keep trying, and we should all do that. But if there is something I have learned very specifically and strongly in the past six years, it is that the unconditional love our Father in Heaven has for us is for this moment and for *always.* It is not going away, and we are deserving of it this very second. Through my prayers, I have come to know without doubt that each one of us is worth it. Yes, even me. And, yes, even you.

* * *

Furthermore, I've learned that it is our privilege to wait upon the Lord. There are many things we will not understand about this life, and we will often not know the *why* of some trials. But I absolutely know that through any trial, we can *always* know and trust the Way.

Corrie Ten Boom shares a beautiful experience in her book *The Hiding Place*. She writes about being on a train with her father and asking him a serious, grown-up question. The conversation follows:

> [My father] turned to look at me, as he always did when answering a question, but to my surprise he said nothing.
>
> At last he stood up, lifted his traveling case from the rack over our heads, and set it on the floor.
>
> "Will you carry it off the train, Corrie?" he said.
>
> I stood up and tugged at it. It was crammed with the watches and spare parts he had purchased that morning.
>
> "It's too heavy," I said.
>
> "Yes," he said, "and it would be a pretty poor father who would ask his little girl to carry such a load. It's the same way, Corrie, with knowledge. Some knowledge is too heavy for children. When you are older and stronger, you can bear it. For now you must trust me to carry it for you."[33]

There are times when we will not understand; in fact, we often may not understand. And we have to trust that our Heavenly Father knows when the knowledge is too heavy for His child to bear. There will come a time when we are old enough and strong enough, but until then, what a wonderful thought that we can trust Him to carry it for us. That He *will* carry it for us. Like the prophet Nephi, we can say we do not know the meaning of all things, but we do know God loves his children.[34] That knowledge is all we need.

I'm so grateful to have been taught that if we wait and trust and act and have faith in the One who is worthy and able to bring us peace and deliverance and joy, He will finish our story to our great good and that waiting is

---

33 Corrie Ten Boom, *The Hiding Place* (Peabody, MA: Hendrickson Publishers, 2009), 29.

34 See 1 Nephi 11:17.

a privilege because there are things we learn in that pause that we cannot learn in any other way. One of the things I have learned in the past six years of waiting on the Lord is that sometimes our situation does not change but we do. And that is enough.

* * *

I came to fully understand the reality and extent of the Savior's love and grace one week near the end of our time in Boston. At the time, I was not only dealing with loneliness but also with several unexpected health issues. My struggle came after many weeks of asking for and not receiving answers from medical professionals. Finally, I asked my husband for a blessing, and in it I was reassured that this was not something I had chosen or that I could fix myself. I needed to lean on my Heavenly Father and Savior, be easy on myself, and know that it would pass. These thoughts and many others throughout the blessing touched my heart deeply.

Just three days later, on Sunday, I made my way to church with our five children. I was feeling like myself again and was deeply grateful. The meeting began, and I was focused on trying to listen and keeping the children quiet. As the priesthood holders blessed the sacrament and began passing the bread and water, I tried hard to keep my thoughts away from any noise or movement around me—I tried to focus on my Savior.

Then, suddenly, with incredible intensity, a revelation came to me. I realized all over again that my Savior, the Redeemer of the world, had atoned for my sins. But in addition, I suddenly knew that Jesus Christ had felt every feeling of discouragement, suffocation, and sadness exactly as I had felt them the previous week. Every single bit of them. *And He didn't have to.* In this particular case, no one had done anything wrong. I had not sinned, and, of course, He was perfect. But He still went through every second of what I was going through because He loved me, because He knew I would have to pass through it, and because He wanted to be able to comfort me exactly how I needed comfort. What that realization did to my heart and the gratitude it filled me with was indescribable, and it has stuck with me ever since then.

This story I shared happens to be mine, but the realization that came to my mind and heart applies to each one of us individually.

* * *

The last six years have taught me so much. Even with the hardship, I can honestly say I would not change anything that has happened to me, because I have come to know that there is not a trial in this life, including heartbreaking and challenging loneliness, that can keep us from happiness and peace in *this* world. In the words of one of my favorite hymns:

> When through the deep waters I call thee to go,
> The rivers of sorrow shall not thee o'erflow,
> For I will be with thee, thy troubles to bless, . . .
> And sanctify to thee thy deepest distress.[35]

Oh, how I know—nothing doubting—that Jesus is the Christ, the Son of God, the promised Messiah, the Prince of Peace, our Savior and Redeemer. And, oh, how I know He loves us and that His Atonement is enough. It is *more* than enough to get us through every challenge, every trial, every moment of grief, every bit of loneliness. Elder Holland testified, "The Lord has 'graven thee upon the palms of [His] hands' (Isaiah 49:16), permanently written right there in scar tissue with Roman nails as the writing instrument."[36]

In the Doctrine and Covenants, we are told, "For I will go before your face. I will be on your right hand and on your left, and my Spirit shall be in your hearts, and mine angels round about you, to bear you up."[37] How incredible is that promise! It is reason enough to lighten the loneliness and be of good cheer, for truly, "God shall be with [us] forever and ever."[38]

---

35 "How Firm a Foundation," *Hymns*, no. 85.

36 "Lessons from Liberty Jail," CES Fireside, September 7, 2008, in *BYU Speeches*.

37 D&C 84:88.

38 D&C 122:9

Part VII: Doing More

16
Examples of Strength: History Has Shown We All Can Do Hard Things

by Michelle Leonard

I can do all things through Christ which strengtheneth me.[39]

"YOU ARE A SURVIVOR TOO" was the thought that came to me one morning as I was making my bed. Uncertain if I had understood the voice correctly, I sat down to ponder what I thought I had heard, and I have been thinking about it ever since.

For months, I had been reading, studying, and thinking about amazing women in my life and in the Church who had overcome some very hard trials and grown closer to God in the process—my mother, friends, women in the scriptures, women from Church history, and even Stephanie Nielson, a young mom and blogger who had survived a terrible plane crash.

They hadn't just survived these difficulties; they had turned to God, and He had given them peace, patience, love, forgiveness, strength, and the ability to overcome. I wondered how they had done it and how some continued to do it. And I thought about how far I still had to go and the many instances where I kept coming up short.

I had never considered myself to be anywhere near the same caliber as these women who lived by faith and trusted in God. Yet this voice was telling me that in spite of my own feelings of inadequacy, in spite of my own weaknesses, my own sins, my own sense of failure, I too had survived some great trials because I had prayed and turned to the Lord—and the Lord had carried me through them.

* * *

My challenges and trials hadn't made the news or Church publications, but God knew them. He knew me, and He helped me—even when I didn't recognize it.

---

39 Philippians 4:13.

I believe God helps everyone. Perhaps in what we feel is our greatest agony or inadequacy or nightmare, we are closest to God—even when we don't recognize He is there with us. He can help us, even as Elder Jeffrey R. Holland said: "You can have sacred, revelatory, profoundly instructive experience with the Lord. . . . *in the most miserable experiences of your life*—in the worst settings, while enduring the most painful injustices, when facing the most insurmountable odds and opposition you have ever faced."[40] Just like God answered Joseph Smith's prayer in a filthy and seemingly inhumane Liberty Jail, He answers our prayers in the worst settings too.

* * *

A man brought his ill son to Jesus Christ and asked, "If thou canst do any thing, have compassion on us and help us." Christ answered, "If thou canst believe, all things are possible to him that believeth." And the father cried out tearfully, "Lord, I believe; help thou mine unbelief."[41]

As a high school student, I realized one evening that despite my best efforts, I would not be getting an academic scholarship to college. I was devastated, sad, and angry. I went into my room and began crying and even praying. That scholarship had been a priority and life goal for me to that point, and now I didn't know what I would do.

After a few minutes, I felt and heard the words, "Don't you trust me?"

I stopped and was humbled. Trust and belief in God's ability to help me was not something that came easily for me, but as Sister Sheri L. Dew said, "We sometimes tend to define unbelievers as apostates or agnostics. But perhaps that definition is far too narrow. What about those of us who have received a witness of the divinity of the Savior and yet deep in our hearts don't believe He will help us? We believe He'll help others— President Hinckley, the Quorum of the Twelve, the stake Relief Society president—but not us."[42]

We are told in the scriptures that we should not put our trust in armies, riches, professions, or possessions; we are even told not to lean unto our own understanding: "Trust in the Lord with all thine heart; and lean not

40 "Lessons from Liberty Jail," CES Fireside, September 7, 2008.
41 Mark 9:22–24.
42 "This Is a Test. It Is Only a Test," *Ensign*, July 2000.

unto thine own understanding. In all thy ways acknowledge him, and he shall direct thy paths."[43]

What does it mean to trust in the Lord? Elder Dallin H. Oaks explained, "The first principle of the gospel is faith in the Lord Jesus Christ. Faith means trust—trust in God's will, trust in His way of doing things, and trust in His timetable. . . . Faith and trust in the Lord give us the strength to accept and persist, whatever happens in our lives."[44] This trust is a belief that God knows what is best for us and when it is best for us, whether it is marriage, death, employment, a calling, or even an assignment to speak in church.

Do we really trust the Savior? Do we not only believe in His divine identity and mission but also in His power to heal us and change us personally? Brother Stephen E. Robinson said, "Unfortunately . . . many of us just don't trust the Savior. We believe in him, but we don't *trust* him. We get so frightened and intimidated, so horrified, by our own imperfections that we don't see how he can possibly save us from them, and we lose faith. . . . Many fear that if they commit themselves to him and try to live the gospel loyally and faithfully, they will miss something important that the world has to offer."[45]

Brother Robinson shared the experience his wife had when she "died to spiritual things." She was burned out. After he asked her for two weeks what was wrong, she finally responded, "I can't do it anymore. I can't lift it. My load is just too heavy. I can't do all the things I'm supposed to do." She rattled off several tasks, such as having scripture study, doing genealogy, and not yelling at her kids. She said, "I've finally admitted to myself that I can't make it to the celestial kingdom, so why should I break my back trying?" Then he asked her if she had a testimony, and she said, "Of course I do—that's what's so terrible. I know the gospel is true, I just can't live up to it." After several hours, they realized what the problem was. She did not understand the core of the gospel, the Atonement of Christ. She was trying to save herself. She believed in Christ, but she didn't understand why He was the Savior for her personally. She felt the demands but didn't feel any of the joy and relief the Savior could bring. [46]

---

43 Proverb 3:5–6.

44 "Timing," *Ensign*, Oct. 2003.

45 *Believing Christ: The Parable of the Bicycle and Other Good News* (Salt Lake City: Deseret Book, 1992), 23.

46 Robinson, *Believing Christ*, 15–17.

I am grateful for Brother Robinson's insight, as that was how I saw the Savior, as a measuring stick, a perfect example, not as the living being who could and would ease my burdens, forgive me, and allow me to forgive and heal.

No matter what our ability to follow rules and commandments, we all need the Savior. None of us can save ourselves. The gospel of Jesus Christ is good news, not a guilt trip. God doesn't want us to go through the motions or be Sunday Christians or serve because we have to. He wants us to want it in our hearts. Above all else, He wants our hearts, just as it says in Proverbs 3:5: "Trust in the Lord with all thine heart; and lean not unto thine own understanding."

When our son Jack was born, he was diagnosed with a heart problem that required immediate surgery. His pulmonary valve was almost completely closed. It opened my eyes to how severely dangerous a hard and closed heart is; likewise, a hard, closed heart can hurt us spiritually. The Lord wants me to soften my heart and trust Him and His will. In fact, the Lord always requires us to give Him a broken heart and contrite spirit (see D&C 64:34). Hard hearts hurt us both physically and spiritually.

* * *

The New Testament is filled with stories of people who came to Jesus asking for a blessing and for healing. Sometimes thousands followed Him as He taught and blessed and healed.

One woman believed but didn't dare speak to Jesus. She had "an issue of blood twelve years" that doctors could not treat.[47] What had she been doing for more than a decade? During much, if not all, of that time, she was isolated from others, being considered unclean. Yet she used her money and resources to try to get better, ultimately waiting upon the Lord. Even though improved health didn't come after two or five or even ten years, she had faith that she would and could be healed.

She believed in the power of Jesus Christ. She believed in His ability to heal her personally. In her humility, uncleanliness, and quest for social solace, this woman came from behind and reached out to Him. She didn't seek a public blessing; she didn't ask to be healed; she didn't even want to be noticed. She just wanted to be made well. When Jesus asked who had touched Him, she came forward with fear and trembling and told

---

47 Mark 5:25.

Him what had happened. She was afraid she had done something wrong, but Christ said to her, "Daughter, thy faith hath made thee whole; go in peace."[48]

Our faith in the Atonement of Jesus Christ allows us to go in peace and be made whole. The Atonement is not just something for sinners; it is also for the Saint striving to do what is right, as Elder David A. Bednar said:

> Most of us know that when we do wrong things, we need help to overcome the effects of sin in our lives. The Savior has paid the price and made it possible for us to become clean through His redeeming power. Most of us clearly understand that the Atonement is for sinners. I am not so sure, however, that we know and understand that the Atonement is also for saints—for good men and women who are obedient, worthy, and conscientious and who are striving to become better and serve more faithfully. We may mistakenly believe we must make the journey from good to better and become a saint all by ourselves, through sheer grit, willpower, and discipline, and with our obviously limited capacities. . . .
>
> I suspect that many Church members are much more familiar with the nature of the redeeming and cleansing power of the Atonement than they are with the strengthening and enabling power. It is one thing to know that Jesus Christ came to earth to *die* for us—that is fundamental and foundational to the doctrine of Christ. But we also need to appreciate that the Lord desires, through His Atonement and by the power of the Holy Ghost, to *live* in us—not only to direct us but also to empower us.[49]

Until she was in her thirties and had experienced a great disappointment, Sister Sheri L. Dew said she thought the Atonement was only for the sinner. During this trying time, she prayed and fasted and attended the temple. Scriptures took on new meaning to her. She said:

> What I learned was not only that the Lord *could* help me but that He *would*. Me. A regular, farm-grown member of

---

48 Mark 5:34.
49 "The Atonement and the Journey of Mortality," *Ensign*, May 2012.

the Church with no fancy titles or spectacular callings. It was during that agonizing period that I began to discover how magnificent, penetrating, and personal the power of the Atonement is. I pleaded with God to change my circumstances, because I believed I could never be happy until He did. Instead, He changed my heart. I asked Him to take away my burden, but He strengthened me so I could bear my burdens with ease (see Mosiah 24:15). I had always been a believer, but I'm not sure I had understood what, or who, it was I believed in.[50]

* * *

Do I believe in a God who will answer my prayers? Do I believe today that Jesus Christ can and will heal me from my feelings of inadequacy and discouragement, as well as from my sins? Do I believe He can strengthen me? Do I see His hand in my life? Do I believe God knows me and loves me?

We are taught from Primary age that we are children of God, but not until recently did I *feel* it was true, that God knew me, that I was His daughter, that I mattered to Him. As President Dieter F. Uchtdorf said: "No matter where you live, no matter how humble your circumstances, how meager your employment, how limited your abilities, how ordinary your appearance, or how little your calling in the Church may appear to you, you are not invisible to your Heavenly Father. He loves you."[51] God loves us and answers our prayers.

Because we know this, how do we increase our trust and improve our relationship with Him? Perhaps we felt closer to God in the past, when we were younger, on our mission, going through a particular trial or calling—but can we feel so now? And why don't we sometimes see and feel God in our lives? Is it because of discouragement and guilt, the burden of sin, or not feeling good enough or doing enough?

Guilt is what keeps us from feeling God, Elder Bruce D. Porter said in a stake conference address: "Burdens of sins, shortcomings and feeling that we aren't good enough or doing enough weigh many saints down," he said. "But Christ came to remove guilt from us, not give us more

---

50 Sheri L. Dew, "This Is a Test. It is Only a Test," *Ensign*, July 2000.
51 "You Matter to Him," *Ensign*, Nov. 2011.

guilt."[52] We do not have to do everything on our own. We can rely on Him. Through prayer, our guilt can be swept away just as it was for Enos. We are saved by the mercy of God, not by our merits.

If we feel distant from God, it could be that we are hurt, angry, too busy, or even too lazy. Maybe we are going through the motions. Maybe we are trying and not seeing or feeling a difference. It could be that we don't feel worthy or that we need to forgive. Maybe this is the closest we have ever felt to God. There are also times when the Lord is slow to hearken to our prayers because we have been slow to hearken to His counsel. The distance may come because we are trying to save ourselves by our works and not trusting Christ and the power of His Atonement. And maybe the problem is that because we are relatively good at following rules we think we are righteous enough.

If we don't see God in our lives, perhaps it is because we are distracted by the things of the world. We look at others and see what we lack instead of being thankful to God for our current situation. And in our ingratitude, we don't recognize that He is there. We can even pray, study the scriptures, and go to church but still not recognize His love and guidance. We can ask ourselves: Do I recognize when the Lord has helped me? Do I allow these small thoughts of goodness—thoughts of God—to change me? Or do I discount them, waiting for some larger answer or miracle? Do I deny the Lord's hand in my life because He sends a simple thought instead of a great miracle? Do I deny what I have been given even though the source of power behind the thought is the same source as the miracle?

Elder Neal A. Maxwell said, "God does not send thunder if a still, small voice is enough."[53] I think many times I'm looking for the thunder, or at least the storm clouds, when I usually already have the simple answers I need. Elder Maxwell also said, "You and I have divine promptings all the time encouraging us to do good, but we often deflect them instead of doing [them]. Promptings for us to do good come from the Holy Ghost. These promptings nudge us further along the straight and narrow path of discipleship. The natural man doesn't automatically think of doing good. It isn't natural."[54] I realize I can and do receive guidance and inspiration from God. I can do what He wants me to do,

---

52 New York stake conference (New York City, NY), personal notes, April 8, 2012.
53 "Notwithstanding My Weakness," *Ensign*, Nov. 1976.
54 "The Pathway of Discipleship," *Ensign*, Sept. 1998.

which may be different from what others do, and I can follow the thought to help myself and others.

* * *

When I was in college, my parents gave me a car to use that we named the Boat. It was an old, huge, blue Buick, and it seemed like its big doors could take out a compact car. There was no air conditioning or power steering, and the brakes didn't work well. On top of all that, the car didn't drive well, and it often overheated. When I wanted to go home from Brigham Young University to Davis County, I would call my parents in advance, tell them the route I was taking, make sure I had food, and turn up the radio to drown out the many noises the old car made. And I would pray my way to Salt Lake—especially over the point of the mountain, crossing from Utah County into Salt Lake County. I was always grateful when I arrived home without incident.

Fast-forward a few years to when I bought my first new car. It was small, it had an automatic heating and cooling system, the engine worked, it was quiet, it had antilock brakes and good tires, and it was reliable. One day as I was driving to work past the point of the mountain, I had this thought: *When is the last time I prayed my way to Salt Lake?* I realized it had been quite a while. Somehow I mistakenly determined I didn't need God now; I had a reliable car. How wrong I was to think that way.

The scriptures say, "And whatsosever ye shall ask the Father in my name, which is right, believing that ye shall receive, behold it shall be given unto you."[55]

Prayer opens hearts and brings peace and the power of God into our lives. I realized this even more powerfully as I learned more about Stephanie Nielson, whose life changed one terrible day in 2008 when her small plane crashed and she was burned on 80 percent of her body. Throughout this miraculous experience, she prayed. During her months in the hospital, she prayed. One time, she said, "Heavenly Father, please help me through this. Please help our children." Then the song "A Child's Prayer" came to her mind, and she wondered if Heavenly Father was really there and if He heard and answered every child's prayer. She said she sang the song out loud over and over. And then she prayed for hours. It was through the process of prayer that she realized God doesn't always

---

55 3 Nephi 18:20.

swoop in to make everything better. Sometimes we have to take an active role in our progression, and then He will do His part.[56]

* * *

But Jesus beheld them, and said unto them, with men this is impossible; but with God all things are possible.[57]

Women throughout the last 150 years have sacrificed, prayed, and worked to further God's kingdom on earth. Time and again these women have known they could go to God in prayer and He would provide. And He has. They have cast their burdens on the Lord and felt relief and strength beyond their own capacity. They have exercised faith and developed spiritual gifts. They have dreamed dreams and witnessed healings. Above all, they have known the heavens aren't closed and have relied on God. They have done what they could and let the Lord help with the rest. He has been with them, perhaps even when they haven't thought He has been. Their faith has been evident in the things they have accomplished.

Consider the realities facing these women:

Abigail Smith Abbott suffered through the death of her husband and much illness as she worked to provide for her family and grow her own garden, and she was blessed with food when her family most needed it.[58]

Sarah De Armon Pea Rich exercised faith and witnessed the power of the Lord on her journey west. She nursed a young motherless boy, George Patten, who traveled with them. And when George became so ill that everyone thought he would die, Sarah prayed and received revelation to know how to save his life. When her husband, Charles, asked how the boy was doing, Sarah said, "Come and see; the boy looked at him and smiled which astonished Charles so much that he turned to me [Sarah] and said, 'What has caused such a change?' I said to him prayer and faith and hope in our Father in Heaven. So, I told my husband what I had done and how humble I felt while praying to the Lord to spare the boy's life."[59]

Emmeline B. Wells was an educated and gifted writer who left her teaching profession in New England amidst ridicule to join the Church

---

56 *Heaven Is Here: An Incredible Story of Hope, Triumph, and Everyday Joy* (New York: Hyperion, 2012), e-book, chap 25.

57 Matthew 19:26.

58 See Richard E. Turley Jr. and Brittany A. Chapman, *Women of Faith in the Latter Days*, Vol. 1:1775–1820 (Salt Lake City: Deseret Book, 2011), 7.

59 *Women of Faith*, 281.

in 1842. She and her new husband and his parents moved to Nauvoo to be near the Prophet. Within two years, when Emmeline was seventeen years old, the Prophet was murdered, her in-laws apostatized, her one and only son died a few weeks after birth, and her husband left to find work and later died. She outlived three husbands and three children. She was a journalist, poet, and editor of the *Woman's Exponent* for more than thirty-nine years and the fifth general Relief Society president. She was an advocate of woman's suffrage and led national groups on women's issues. She led a grain saving program, which provided sustenance during a severe drought in Southern Utah as well as after an earthquake and fire in San Francisco in 1906, and a famine in China in 1907. The stored wheat also provided nourishment for thousands of people during World War I when the Relief Society sold two hundred thousand bushels to the United States government.

Emmeline struggled with depression. She had a public, accomplished self and another somewhat fragile, emotional self. She often took to her bed with a nervous disorder or spells of despondency. She said: "I never remember to have had so many disagreeable feelings in one evening in all my life. . . . I was alone feeling to[o] gloomy even to write[,] crying most of the time, and my heart nearly bursting, I shall never forget it if I live to be a thousand years old; I never remember of suffering like that before, with the same feelings, O how hard it is to endure unto the end, I am not sure if it be possible for me or not[;] sometimes I think I have to[o] much to bear."[60]

As Relief Society president, Emmeline worried that many sisters weren't relying on the spiritual aspects of the gospel but on outward, temporal appearances. She urged members to hold fast to their covenants. She wrote, "I have desired with all my heart to do those things that would advance women in moral and spiritual as well as educational work and tend to the rolling on of the work of God upon the earth."[61]

Sahar Qumsiyeh is a Palestinian Christian who lived in Israel for many years. She was born in Jerusalem and grew up near Bethlehem. She attended BYU, and while there, she investigated the Church and was later baptized. However, her family and friends didn't approve when she returned home. In

---

60 In Carol Cornwall Madsen, "Emmeline B. Wells: Romantic Rebel," *Supporting Saints: Life Stories of Nineteenth Century Mormons*, ed. Donald Q. Cannon and David J. Whittaker (Provo, UT: Brigham Young University, Religious Studies Center, 1985), 305–41.

61 *Daughters in My Kingdom: The History and Work of Relief Society*, 57.

spite of the incessant and constant verbal harassment, Sahar found ways to still attend church. She would evade the Israeli checkpoints and eventually the separation walls to get to the small branch she attended. She did it for twelve years, and she considered each Sabbath day attendance at church a miracle. She firmly believed that when she was obedient, God would bless her.[62]

We read these remarkable stories and ask how they did it and how they survived. The answer is that they did it with the help of the Lord. They did it *with* Him. They prayed in faith and acted on that direction. They recognized God's hand in their lives and thanked Him for the privilege. God required the best of them—even all they had—and they gave it, and He made up the difference.

* * *

Stories from scriptures and throughout our history give us a brief glimpse of women who chose to have faith and believe in God instead of doubt, women who chose to pray instead of turn in silence from Him, women who chose to act on the direction they received. They chose to believe God would provide. They chose faith.

I have learned through these women that the heavens are not closed. In all moments, God can be there with us, for us, and even in us to enable us with strength and the power to do His will. Prayer opens our hearts and heaven's door. With God, nothing is impossible.

We too can be comforted in Christ. Through our trials, we can say, as a friend did, "We have learned as is described in Romans 8 that nothing will separate us from the love of Christ, not death, infertility, cancer, brain tumors, depression, fear, sorrow, or things present, or things past; nothing will separate us from the love of Christ."[63]

I am grateful for the many people I know—friends and family—who, despite challenges, trials, and injustices, still look to God. They still believe in Him as a loving Father, in His plan in the Atonement of Jesus Christ, and in the possibility and hope of forgiveness, healing, and eternal life.

Women disciples of the past played a role, and women of the present can too—women who work, who blog, who are single, who are married,

---

62 See "Peace through Conflict," The Mormon Women Project, November 17, 2010, retrieved from http://www.mormonwomen.com/2010/11/17/peace-through-conflict/.

63 Christina Parkinson, BYU Women's Conference lecture, April 29, 2011.

who are divorced, who are disabled, who are depressed, who are widowed, who are alone, who are ill, who are fit, who are professional, who are intellectual, who are simple, who are young, who are not so young, who are happy, who are tired, women who have soft hearts.

With the help of the Lord, *I* can do hard things too, not just people from the scriptures or people from Church history, or people who have had catastrophic accidents happen to them. I too can pray. I too can receive revelation. I too can have faith in a living Jesus Christ and can do hard things with His help. God knows me. I am His daughter. He has a plan for me. That plan might be different from someone else's plan, but the Lord can and will guide all of us if we let Him and if we choose to recognize Him and give thanks.

We as women have similar responsibilities throughout the world, and not everyone will understand our decisions, but we can exercise faith and trust in God to provide for us in the present as He provided for faithful women in the past.

The beauty and miracle of the gospel of Jesus Christ is the belief in a personal, *living* God, a God who can comfort and guide us individually. Women have done things that at times haven't been logical, but they have prayed and followed that Spirit of God and survived. They have looked to God and lived.

We have that same charge today. We don't have to go it alone. We can partner with the Divine.[64] We too can look to God and live.

---

[64] See Sheri L. Dew, "We Are Not Alone," *Ensign*, Nov. 1998.

17
Adversity: The Mark of Gold upon Our Souls
By Shelly Locke

ELDER GLENN L. PACE, OF the Seventy, said, "Into each of our lives come golden moments of adversity. This painful friend breaks our hearts, drops us to our knees, and makes us realize we are nothing without our Lord and Savior. This friend makes us plead all the night long for reassurance and into the next day and sometimes for weeks and months. But, ultimately, just as surely as the day follows the night, as we remain true and faithful, this strange friend, adversity, leads straight into the outstretched arms of our Savior."[65]

There never has been such a time as this, a time when men's hearts fail them more, for we think not of our God or what could be if we were inextricably linked to one another for our good. We may not think of it, but the fact still remains that we *are* linked for good or bad, and the character of God *is* in us all. He is our Father, and He loves us more than mortal tongue can tell. He also blesses us in the most extraordinary ways if we but look to find His blessings one by one. Likewise, He asks that we love and bless each other. This great love is the essence of all life, and the more we give by love, the more we receive; it is one eternal round.

These blessings and duties hold great importance because they prepare us for the trials of life, which through our actions can become *blessings* that move us toward the throne of God—their lessons learned become priceless gems that give deeper meaning to our loving interaction with God. They become the price we pay to *know* our God, and as we do this, they refine us, they give us understanding, and they make us more like Him. If we manage our trials wisely, they become our friend, the means by which the answers to life's mysteries will come.

---

65 "Spiritual Revival," *Ensign*, Nov. 1992.

All trials and adversity have a purpose. We were placed on this earth to gain experience, and the more we learn, the brighter shines our light and the greater the good we can do. We often focus on the hardship of the trial, but it is not so much what the trial is but our response to it that matters. When we face what comes our way with grace and faith, it makes a final mark upon our lives—not a scar or a deep wound but, rather, a mark of *fire*, where the Refiner touches our lives and burns away the dross, leaving instead the mark of gold upon our souls. Our trials do not define us, but the way we overcome them does.

* * *

The peace God bestows on us when we understand our place in the great scheme of things upon the earth makes us stronger so we can endure the journey we are on. This peace opens our hearts and allows us to become instruments in God's hands, beacons of all hope, bastions of all joy.

When we feel this peace, we have a greater capacity to love, which love changes lives for good and heals people. It is a miraculous power, and it is incredible to think that God has room within His heart for each one who comes before His altar to lay their burden down and then take it up again with the power, light, and knowledge that make it so much easier to bear.

There is not one thing He does not know of suffering, of longing, of need both deep and long. He has gone before, tread the winepress alone, and He now invites us to become one with Him.

Truly, all things *are* possible with God. That is His blessing—that we can accomplish all things with Him at our side, forevermore in love, knowing we are His beloved children and He will never forsake us.

This is the essence of pure joy, and knowing this, we can go forth saying, "My God lives and loves His children and blesses us to overcome all things, that we may be like Him in truth and love forevermore."

Letter to the Reader

I HAVE FREQUENTLY BEEN ASKED why I compiled this book. The truth is it is God's, not so much mine. I resisted writing it for a long time. My responses to His promptings sounded a little like, "But there are already so many books in the world, so should I really write one more?" However, the promptings kept coming, and so did the stories that needed to be told, including some of my own hard things that hadn't happened when I first set out to write this book. With my second rejection letter from a publisher, I almost put the book away in a drawer, deciding it was a growing experience but that it wouldn't come to print. But doing hard things with God means trusting His timing and knowing all these experiences will work together for my good. Because I didn't give up on this book, it stands as a witness of countless tender mercies and miracles.

Reading the stories of these women overwhelms me with gratitude and awe at God's hand in the timing of this book. Each writer pushed through the emotions that came with sharing such personal stories. Their courage and love for you, the reader, kept them committed to the process to the end. Their individual experiences were profound, and combined, they tell an even bigger story of faith. After my sister's suicide, I felt even more passionately that connections can be a matter of life or death and that I urgently needed to get these stories into anyone's hands who needed them.

One dream for this book is that LDS and non-LDS readers alike will find it and gain strength in the shared experiences of acting with faith in God during difficult circumstances. I invite you to share this book with others. I also invite you to visit the companion website at www.icanwithgod.com, where you can get to know the women in this book better and share your own personal story of testimony and strength.

With love,
Ganel-Lyn Condie

About the Author

GANEL-LYN KNOWS ANYTHING IS POSSIBLE with God. She never dreamed of writing when she graduated from Arizona State University with a BS in elementary education and psychology, yet she has become an award-winning journalist and was editor of *Wasatch Woman* magazine. She has interviewed well-known public figures, including Cokie Roberts and Richard Paul Evans, and has a talent for sharing other people's stories. She loves being a wife and mother and will always be grateful for her family. They and her faith helped her heal from a chronic illness and years of chemotherapy treatments for a heart condition. They've truly been instruments in the Lord's hands in many other ways. Because of her experiences, Ganel-Lyn has a passion for creating balance, organization, and spirituality in life and at home. She has discovered the joy of sharing experiences with others through her newspaper column, consulting, public speaking, and her website, www.ganellyn.com.